GOD'S
SURVIVAL GUIDE

GOD'S
SURVIVAL GUIDE

A HANDBOOK
FOR CRISIS TIMES
IN YOUR LIFE

TABLE OF CONTENTS

After the Crisis

INTRODUCTION

If you're reading this book, you're undoubtedly searching for solutions. Your life, like every human life, is a collection of stories: some grand, some not-so-grand, some disappointing, and some tragic. During the good times, you will celebrate. But, when life takes a tragic turn, you will ask tough questions that defy easy answers. This book is intended to help.

Perhaps you have sought solutions on your own; perhaps friends and family members have tried to help; perhaps you have almost given up hope. Wherever you are, no matter how difficult your circumstances, God has a plan for you, a plan that offers comfort, perspective, and peace. That plan is contained in His Holy Word, and this book is designed to help you find it.

At the end of the day, when no one else can comfort you, God can. In the hours before dawn, when you toss and turn and wrestle with worries about a broken past or an uncertain future, God offers a peace unlike any other. But if you're like most of us, finding God's peace isn't always easy, especially when your heart is broken.

This book touches upon 45 topics, issues such as rejection and disappointment, failure and hardship, depression and grief. In addition to scriptural resources, the text also contains quote-worthy ideas from notable Christian thinkers.

So, if you're struggling to find solutions to life's toughest questions, don't give up. Instead, keep searching for wisdom, starting with God's wisdom. When you do, you'll discover the strength, the comfort, and the assurance that only He can give.

PART I

HOW WE THINK

Thoughts are things . . . powerful things. Our thoughts have the power to lift us up or to hold us back. Our prevailing attitudes have the power to create happiness or dissatisfaction, joy or pain, peace or stress, success or failure.

In Part I of God's Survival Guide, we consider ways to think more carefully, more optimistically, more realistically, and more faithfully.

ACCEPTING THE PAST

Some of life's greatest roadblocks are not the ones we see through the windshield; they are, instead, the roadblocks that seem to fill the rearview mirror. Because we are imperfect human beings who lack perfect control over our thoughts, we may allow ourselves to become "stuck" in the past—even though we know better. Instead of focusing our thoughts and energies on the opportunities of today, we may allow painful memories to fill our minds and sap our strength. We simply can't seem to let go of our pain, so we relive it again and again . . . with predictably unfortunate consequences. Thankfully, God has other plans.

Philippians 3:13, 14 instructs us to focus on the future, not the past: "One thing I do, forgetting those things which are behind and reaching forward to those things which are ahead, I press toward the goal for the prize of the upward call of God in Christ Jesus" (NKJV). Yet for many of us, focusing on the future is difficult indeed. Why? Part of the problem has to do with forgiveness. When we find ourselves focusing too intently on the past, it's a sure sign that we need to focus, instead, on a more urgent need: the need to forgive. Until we thoroughly and completely forgive those who have hurt us—and until we completely forgive ourselves for our own mistakes and shortcomings—we are never fully free from the past.

Focusing too intently on the past is, almost without exception, futile. No amount of anger or bitterness can change what happened yesterday. Tears can't change the past; regrets can't change it. Our worries won't change the past, and neither will our complaints. Simply put, the past is, and always will be, the past. Forever.

Can you summon both the courage and the wisdom to accept your past and move on with your life? Can you accept the reality that yesterday—and all the yesterdays before it—are gone? And, can you entrust all those yesterdays to God? Hopefully you can.

Once you have made peace with your past, you are free to become fully engaged in the present. And when you become fully engaged in the present, you are then free to build a better future for yourself and your loved ones.

If you've endured a difficult past, learn from it, but don't live in it. Instead, build your future on a firm foundation of trust and forgiveness: trust in your Heavenly Father, and forgiveness for all His children, including yourself. Give all your yesterdays to God, and celebrate this day with hope in your heart and praise on your lips. Your Creator intends to use you in wonderful, unexpected ways if you let Him. But first, God wants you to make peace with your past . . . and He wants you to do it now.

*The Lord says, "Forget what happened before, and
do not think about the past. Look at the new thing
I am going to do. It is already happening. Don't you see it?
I will make a road in the desert and rivers in the dry land."*

ISAIAH 43:18, 19 NCV

*And we know that all things work together for good to those
who love God, to those who are the called
according to His purpose.*

ROMANS 8:28 NKJV

*But also I am writing a new command to you, and you can see
its truth in Jesus and in you, because the darkness is passing
away, and the true light is already shining.*

1 JOHN 2:8 NCV

*But may the God of all grace, who called us to
His eternal glory by Christ Jesus, after you have suffered
a while, perfect, establish, strengthen, and settle you.*

1 PETER 5:10 NKJV

Shake the dust from your past, and move forward
in His promises.

KAY ARTHUR

Leave the broken, irreversible past in God's hands, and
step out into the invincible future with Him.

OSWALD CHAMBERS

We can't just put our pasts behind us.
We've got to put our pasts in front of God.

BETH MOORE

Finish every day and be done with it. You have done what
you could; some blunders and absurdities have crept in;
forget them as soon as you can.

RALPH WALDO EMERSON

Resolutely slam and lock the door on past sin and failure,
and throw away the key.

OSWALD CHAMBERS

Additional Bible Readings

EZEKIEL 36:26; JOHN 14:27; PSALM 51:10; PSALM 118:24

ANGER

Anger is a natural human emotion that is sometimes necessary and appropriate. One example of appropriate anger is found in Matthew 21: "Then Jesus went into the temple of God and drove out all those who bought and sold in the temple, and overturned the tables of the money changers and the seats of those who sold doves" (v. 12 NKJV).

Righteous indignation is an appropriate response to evildoing, but God does not intend that anger should rule our lives. Far from it. God intends that we turn away from anger whenever possible and forgive our neighbors just as we seek forgiveness for ourselves.

Because we are imperfect human beings living among other imperfect human beings, we encounter countless frustrations, some great and some small. On occasion, we, like Jesus, will confront imminent evil, and when we do, we should attempt to respond as He did: vigorously and without reservation. But more often than not, our challenges are much more mundane. We are confronted, not by moneychangers in the temple, but by the inevitable distractions and disappointments of life here on earth: jammed traffic, spilled coffee, and similar inconveniences. Our challenge is this: to display anger when it is appropriate and to rein in our tempers when it is not.

How can we learn to maintain better control over our tempers? By focus, by forgiveness, and by faith. We must learn to focus our thoughts, not on the inevitable disappointments of life, but instead upon the innumerable blessings that God has given us (Philippians 4:8). In other words, we must learn to look carefully at the donut, not the hole. Forgiveness is another tool that we can use to rein in anger. When we forgive others thoroughly and often, we avoid the anger-provoking traps of bitterness and regret. Faith, too, is an antidote to anger. When we allow our faith in God to become the cornerstone and the touchstone of our lives, we cultivate an unwavering trust in the righteousness of His plans. When we do so, we begin to see God's hand as it works in every aspect of our lives—in good times and in hard times—as He uses every circumstance to fulfill His plan for us.

Sometimes we are victims of secondhand anger. We may become angry because someone else is angry. Why? Because anger is a highly contagious emotion. When we spend time with angry people, we, too, tend to become angry. Once again, God's Word offers a solution that doubles as a warning: "Make no friendship with an angry man" (Proverbs 22:24 NKJV).

The next time you are tempted to lose your temper over the minor inconveniences of life, don't. Turn away from angry people and angry thoughts. Turn instead to God. Choose forgiveness instead of hatred; choose acceptance, not regret; let the assurance of God's eternal promises overcome the inevitability of life's fleeting disappointments. When you do, you'll give yourself a priceless gift: the gift of peace. And God will smile.

*Let all bitterness, wrath, anger, clamor, and evil speaking
be put away from you, with all malice.
And be kind to one another, tenderhearted,
forgiving one another, just as God in Christ
forgave you.*

EPHESIANS 4:31, 32 NKJV

*When you are angry, do not sin, and be sure to stop being
angry before the end of the day.
Do not give the devil a way to defeat you.*

EPHESIANS 4:26, 27 NCV

*My dear brothers and sisters, always be willing to listen and
slow to speak. Do not become angry easily, because
anger will not help you live the right kind of life God wants.*

JAMES 1:19, 20 NCV

Don't become angry quickly, because getting angry is foolish.

ECCLESIASTES 7:9 NCV

More Thoughts About . . . ANGER

When you strike out in anger, you may miss
the other person, but you will always hit yourself.

JIM GALLERY

Anger is the noise of the soul; the unseen irritant of
the heart; the relentless invader of silence.

MAX LUCADO

The deadly cancer of anger from which so much harm
grows: It makes us unlike ourselves, makes us like timber
wolves or furies from hell; drives us forth headlong upon
the points of swords, makes us blindly run forth after
other men's destruction as we hasten toward our own ruin.

ST. THOMAS MORE

Forgiveness is the key that unlocks the door of resentment
and the handcuffs of hate. It is a power that breaks
the chains of bitterness and the shackles of selfishness.

CORRIE TEN BOOM

Unrighteous anger feeds the ego and produces
the poison of selfishness in the heart.

WARREN WIERSBE

Additional Bible Readings

COLOSSIANS 3:8; MATTHEW 12:36, 37; PROVERBS 29:22;

PROVERBS 14:29; PSALM 37:7, 8

ANXIETY AND PANIC

We live in a world that sometimes seems to shift beneath our feet. We live in an uncertain world, a world where tragedies can befall even the most godly among us. And we are members of an anxious society, a society in which the changes we face threaten to outpace our abilities to make adjustments. No wonder we sometimes find ourselves beset by feelings of anxiety and panic.

At times, our anxieties may stem from physical causes—chemical imbalances in the brain that result in severe emotional distress or relentless panic attacks. In such cases, modern medicine offers hope to those who suffer. But oftentimes, our anxieties result from spiritual deficits, not physical ones. And when we're spiritually depleted, the best prescription is found not in the medicine cabinet but deep inside the human heart. What we need is a higher daily dose of God's love, God's peace, God's assurance, and God's presence. And how do we acquire these blessings from our Creator? Through prayer, through meditation, through worship, and through trust.

Prayer is a powerful antidote to anxiety; so, too is a regular time of devotional reading and meditation. When we spend quiet moments in the divine presence of our Heavenly Father, we are reminded once again that our troubles are temporary but His love is not.

Worship, like prayer, is another tool that can help us

overcome the worries and doubts of our anxious age. When we worship God sincerely with our words, with our thoughts, with our prayers, and with our deeds, we are blessed. But the reverse is also true: when we fail to worship God, for whatever reason, we forfeit the spiritual gifts that He intends to be ours.

Learning to trust God completely and without reservation is yet another antidote to anxiety. In fact, a fundamental relationship exists between anxiety and trust: the more we trust God, the less anxious we are likely to feel. But once again, the reverse is also true: the less we trust God, the more anxious we are likely to become. When we turn away from God and rely, instead, upon the world for our deliverance, we will be troubled—and rightfully so. The world will disappoint us; God will not.

From time to time, all of us face life-changing personal losses that leave us breathless. When we do, God stands ready to protect us. Psalm 147 promises, "He heals the brokenhearted and bandages their wounds" (v. 3, NCV). When we are troubled, we must call upon God, and, in His own time and according to His own plan, He will heal us.

Are you anxious? Take those anxieties to God. Are you troubled? Take your troubles to Him. Does your world seem to be trembling beneath your feet? Seek protection from the One who cannot be moved. The same God who created the universe will protect you if you ask Him . . . so ask and trust.

God's Word About . . . ANXIETY AND PANIC

When you pass through the waters, I will be with you;
And through the rivers, they shall not overflow you.
When you walk through the fire, you shall not be burned,
Nor shall the flame scorch you. For I am the Lord your God,
The Holy One of Israel, your Savior; I gave Egypt for
your ransom, Ethiopia and Seba in your place.

ISAIAH 43:2, 3 NKJV

Be anxious for nothing, but in everything by prayer and
supplication, with thanksgiving, let your requests be made
known to God; and the peace of God, which surpasses
all understanding, will guard your hearts and
minds through Christ Jesus.

PHILIPPIANS 4:6, 7 NKJV

In the multitude of my anxieties within me,
Your comforts delight my soul.

PSALM 94:19 NKJV

...casting all your care upon Him, for He cares for you.
Be sober, be vigilant; because your adversary the devil walks
about like a roaring lion, seeking whom he may devour.
Resist him, steadfast in the faith, knowing that the same
sufferings are experienced by your brotherhood in the world.
But may the God of all grace, who called us to His eternal glory
by Christ Jesus, after you have suffered a while,
perfect, establish, strengthen, and settle you.

1 PETER 5: 7, 10 NKJV

More Thoughts About . . . ANXIETY AND PANIC

One of the main missions of God is to free us from
the debilitating bonds of fear and anxiety.
God's heart is broken when He sees us so demoralized
and weighed down by fear.

BILL HYBELS

The moment anxious thoughts invade your mind,
go to the Lord in prayer. Look first to God. Then,
you will see the cause of your anxiety in a whole new light.

KAY ARTHUR

The thing that preserves a man from panic is
his relationship to God.

OSWALD CHAMBERS

So often we pray and then fret anxiously, waiting for God
to hurry up and do something. All the while God is waiting
for us to calm down, so He can do something through us.

CORRIE TEN BOOM

Additional Bible Readings

DEUTERONOMY 3:8; LUKE 12: 29-31; PROVERBS 12:25; PSALM 103:2-4;

PSALM 139:23, 24; PSALM 46:10; PSALM 121

BITTERNESS

Are you mired in the quicksand of bitterness or regret? If so, be forewarned: You are not only disobeying your Heavenly Father, you are also wasting your time. The world holds few if any rewards for those who remain angrily focused upon the past injustices. And neither, for that matter, does God.

God's Word is clear. In the 43rd chapter of Isaiah, we read: "The Lord says, 'Forget what happened before, and do not think about the past. Look at the new thing I am going to do. It is already happening. Don't you see it? I will make a road in the desert and rivers in the dry land'" (v. 18, 19 NCV). Yet most of us have great difficulty forgetting "what happened before." Instead of entrusting the past to God's providence, we dwell upon the misfortunes of yesterday. The irony of our shortsightedness is this: By allowing ourselves to become embittered by our disappointments, we inevitably set ourselves up for even more disappointments in the future. Why? Because bitter hearts yield bitter fruits (Luke 6:44, 45).

Being frail, fallible, imperfect human beings, most of us are quick to anger, quick to blame, slow to forgive, and even slower to forget. Yet as Christians, we are commanded to forgive others, just as we, too, have been forgiven. The Bible teaches us that if we judge our brothers and sisters, we, too, will be subject to judgement (Matthew 5:22). Let us refrain, then, from judging our neighbors. Instead, let us forgive them and love them, while leaving their judgement to a far more capable authority: the One who sits on His throne in heaven.

Bitterness is a spiritual sickness that can consume us if we let it. Our challenge, as responsible believers who seek to walk with God, is this: we must train ourselves to think—and to pray—in ways that remove the poison of bitterness from our hearts.

If you are caught up in intense feelings of anger or resentment, you know all too well the destructive power of these emotions. How can you rid yourself of these feelings? First, you must prayerfully ask God to cleanse your heart. Then, you must learn to catch yourself whenever thoughts of bitterness or hatred begin to attack you. In short, you must learn to recognize and to resist negative thoughts before they hijack your emotions.

If there exists even one person—alive or dead—against whom you hold bitter feelings, it's time to forgive. Or, if you are embittered against yourself for some past mistake or shortcoming, it's finally time to forgive yourself and move on. Remember that bitterness is not part of God's plan for you life, so pray, think, and forgive accordingly.

*Indeed it was for my own peace That I had great bitterness;
But You have lovingly delivered my soul from
the pit of corruption, For You have cast
all my sins behind Your back.*

ISAIAH 38:17 NKJV

*Pursue peace with all people, and holiness, without which
no one will see the Lord: looking carefully lest anyone fall short
of the grace of God; lest any root of bitterness springing up
cause trouble, and by this many become defiled.*

HEBREWS 12:14, 15 NKJV

*The heart knows its own bitterness,
And a stranger does not share its joy.*

PROVERBS 14:10 NKJV

Don't become angry quickly, because getting angry is foolish.

ECCLESIASTES 7:9 NCV

More Thoughts About . . . **BITTERNESS**

Give me such love for God and men as will blot out
all hatred and bitterness.

DIETRICH BONHOEFFER

Be so preoccupied with good will that you haven't room
for ill will.

E. STANLEY JONES

Bitterness is the price we charge ourselves for being
unwilling to forgive.

MARIE T. FREEMAN

The recollection of an injury is a rusty arrow and
poison to the soul.

ST. FRANCIS OF PAOLA

Forgiveness is the key which unlocks the door of
resentment and the handcuffs of hatred.
It breaks the chains of bitterness and
the shackles of selfishness.

CORRIE TEN BOOM

Additional Bible Readings

ACTS 8:22, 23; EPHESIANS 4:26, 27, 31, 32; JAMES 3:14; PHILIPPIANS 4:11

DEPRESSION

It has been said, and with good reason, that depression is the common cold of mental illness. Why? Because depression is such a common malady. But make no mistake: depression is a serious condition that, if untreated, can take a terrible toll on individuals and families alike.

The sadness that accompanies any significant loss is an inescapable fact of life. Throughout our lives, all of us must endure the kinds of deep personal losses that leave us struggling to find hope. But in time, we move beyond our grief as the sadness runs its course and gradually abates.

Depression, on the other hand, is a physical and emotional condition that is, in almost all cases, treatable with medication and counseling. Depression is not a disease to be taken lightly. Left untreated, it presents real dangers to patients' physical health and to their emotional wellbeing.

If you find yourself feeling "blue," perhaps it's a logical reaction to the ups and downs of daily life. But if your feelings of sadness have lasted longer than you think they should—or if someone close to you fears that your sadness may have evolved into clinical depression—it's time to seek professional help.

Here are a few simple guidelines to consider as you make decisions about possible medical treatment: 1. If you have persistent urges toward self-destructive behavior, or if feel as though you have lost the will to live, consult a professional counselor or physician immediately. 2. If someone you trust urges you to seek counseling, schedule a session with a professionally trained counselor to evaluate your condition. 3. If you experience persistent and prolonged changes in sleep patterns, or if you experience a significant change in weight (either gain or loss), consult your physician. 4. If you are plagued by consistent, prolonged, severe feelings of hopelessness, consult a physician, a professional counselor, or your pastor.

In the familiar words of John 10:10, Jesus promises, "I have come that they may have life, and that they may have it more abundantly" (NKJV). And in John 15:11, He states, "These things I have spoken to you, that My joy may remain in you, and that your joy may be full." These two passages make it clear: Our Savior intends that we experience lives of joyful abundance through Him. Our duty, as grateful believers, is to do everything we can to receive the joy and abundance that can be ours in Christ—and the term "everything" includes appropriate medical treatment when necessary.

Some days are light and happy, and some days are not. When we face the inevitable dark days of life, we must choose how we will respond. Will we allow ourselves to sink even more deeply into our own sadness, or will we do the difficult work of pulling ourselves out? We bring light to the dark days of life by turning first to God, and then to trusted family members, to friends, and, in some cases, to medical professionals. When we do, the clouds will eventually part, and the sun will shine once more upon our souls.

Answer me speedily, O Lord; My spirit fails! Do not hide
Your face from me, Lest I be like those who go down into
the pit. Cause me to hear Your lovingkindness in the morning,
For in You do I trust; Cause me to know the way in which
I should walk, For I lift up my soul to You.

PSALM 143:7, 8 NKJV

Fear not, for I am with you; Be not dismayed,
for I am your God. I will strengthen you, Yes, I will help you,
I will uphold you with My righteous right hand.

ISAIAH 41:10 NKJV

But those who wait on the Lord Shall renew their strength;
They shall mount up with wings like eagles,
They shall run and not be weary, They shall walk and not faint.

ISAIAH 40:31 NKJV

Weeping may endure for a night, but joy comes in the morning.

PSALM 30:5 NKJV

Emotions we have not poured out in the safe hands of
God can turn into feelings of hopelessness and depression.
God is safe.

BETH MOORE

Some of the best depression blockers are: a strong will
to live, blazing determination, and a sense of purpose.

NORMAN COUSINS

God conquers only what we yield to Him.
Yet, when He does, and when our surrender is complete,
He fills us with a new strength that we could never have
known by ourselves. His conquest is our victory!

SHIRLEY DOBSON

Don't let aridity distress you: perfection has nothing to do
with such things—only with virtues.
Your devotion will come back when you are
least expecting it.

ST. TERESA OF AVILA

Additional Bible Readings

1 PETER 4:12, 13; 2 SAMUEL 22:29-31; ISAIAH 49:16; ISAIAH 51:11;

PHILIPPIANS 4:8; PSALM 23; PSALM 27:4, 5; PSALM 40:1-3A; PSALM 56:8

DISAPPOINTMENTS

From time to time, all of us face life-altering disappointments that leave us breathless. Oftentimes, these disappointments come unexpectedly, leaving us with more questions than answers. But even when we don't have all the answers—or, for that matter, even when we don't seem to have any of the answers—God does. Whatever our circumstances, whether we stand atop the highest mountain or wander through the darkest valley, God is ready to protect us, to comfort us, and to heal us. Our task is to let Him.

Life is a tapestry of events: some grand, some not-so-grand, some disappointing, and some tragic. During the happy times, we are tempted to take our blessings for granted (a temptation that we must resist with all our might). But, during life's difficult days, we discover precisely what we're made of. And more importantly, we discover what our faith is made of.

If your faith is being tested by difficult circumstances, perhaps it's time to ask yourself three important questions: 1. "How does God want me to respond?" 2. "What does God want me to learn?" 3. "Where does God want me to go from here?" When you ask yourself these questions, here are some things to consider:

YOUR RESPONSE

God wants you to respond to life's disappointing moments with an attitude of obedience. No matter how difficult your circumstances, God calls you to obey the instructions that are contained in His Holy Word. He wants to remain hopeful (Psalm 31:24); He instructs you to remain faithful to Him, and He wants you to be courageous (Matthew 8:26). God also expects you to forgive those who have injured you (Matthew 6:14, 15), and He wants you to treat others with kindness and gentleness (Ephesians 4:32). These commandments are often difficult to obey—especially when you feel angry, or hurt—but obey them you must . . . otherwise you invite God's disapproval.

YOUR LESSONS

What does God want you to learn from your disappointments? Plenty! Every disappointing chapter of life has important lessons to teach, but no one can learn those lessons for you—you must learn them for yourself. And with God's help, you will.

Hidden within every disappointment is the potential for personal and spiritual growth. Life's darker days are filled with "teachable moments"—moments that offer unique learning opportunities. During these moments, God has things that He wants to say specifically to you. You, in turn, must make yourself open to His instructions.

Your Future

If you've endured a life-altering disappointment, you may have good reason to ask, "Where do you want me to go from here, Lord?" And you may rest assured that, in time, Your Heavenly Father will answer you. His answer may not come immediately, and it may not come in a way that you expect, but of this you can be certain: if you sincerely ask, God will answer (Matthew 7:7, 8).

Your Heavenly Father has a perfect plan and a chosen path for all of His children, including you. When tough times arrive, you should learn from your experiences and you should prayerfully seek God's guidance for the future. Then, you should get busy with the work at hand—the difficult and rewarding work of overcoming your disappointments. When you do your part, you can be certain that God will do His part. And you can be sure that in time, your loving Heavenly Father will turn your stumbling blocks into stepping stones.

THE NEXT TIME YOU'RE DISAPPOINTED,

DON'T PANIC AND DON'T GIVE UP.

JUST BE PATIENT AND LET GOD REMIND YOU HE'S STILL IN CONTROL.

—

MAX LUCADO

For the Lord is good; His mercy is everlasting,
and His truth endures to all generations.

PSALM 100:5 NKJV

For now we see in a mirror, dimly, but then face to face.
Now I know in part, but then I shall know
just as I also am known.

1 CORINTHIANS 13:12 NKJV

"I say this because I know what I am planning for you,"
says the Lord.
"I have good plans for you, not plans to hurt you.
I will give you hope and a good future."

JEREMIAH 29:11 NCV

There is one thing I always do. Forgetting the past and
straining toward what is ahead, I keep trying to reach
the goal and get the prize for which God called me . . . .

PHILIPPIANS 3:13, 14 NCV

More Thoughts About . . . DISAPPOINTMENTS

Every achievement worth remembering is stained
with the blood of diligence and scarred by
the wounds of disappointment.

CHARLES SWINDOLL

If your hopes are being disappointed just now,
it means that they are being purified.

OSWALD CHAMBERS

The amazing thing is that God follow us into
the blackened ruins of our failed dreams, our misbegotten
mirages, into the house of cards that has collapsed on us
in some way and he speaks, not with the chastisement
we feel we deserve, but of all things, with tenderness.

PAULA RINEHART

You are beaten to earth? Well, well, what's that?
Come up with a smiling face; it's nothing against you to
fall down flat, but to lie there—that's disgrace.

EDMUND VANCE COOKE

Additional Bible Readings

2 CORINTHIANS 7:6; HEBREWS 10:23; PHILIPPIANS 4:13;

PSALM 18:30; ROMANS 8:31

DISCOURAGEMENT

We Christians have many reasons to celebrate. God is in His heaven; Christ has risen, and we are the sheep of His flock. Yet sometimes, even the most devout believers may become discouraged. After all, we live in a world where expectations can be high and demands can be even higher.

When we fail to meet the expectations of others (or, for that matter, the expectations that we have set for ourselves), we may be tempted to abandon hope. But God has other plans. He knows exactly how He intends to use us. Our task is to remain faithful until He does.

When we are discouraged—on those cloudy days when our strength is sapped and our faith is shaken—there exists a source from which we can draw courage and wisdom. That source is God. When we seek to form a more intimate and dynamic relationship with our Creator, He renews our spirits and restores our souls. This promise is made clear Isaiah 40:

Have you not known? Have you not heard? The everlasting God, the Lord, the Creator of the ends of the earth, neither faints nor is weary. His understanding is unsearchable. He gives power to the weak, and to those who have no might He increases strength. Even the youths shall faint and be weary, and the young men shall utterly fall, but those who wait on the Lord Shall renew their strength; they shall mount up with wings like eagles, they shall run and not be weary, they shall walk and not faint." (v. 28-31 NKJV)

God offers us the strength to meet our challenges, and He offers us hope for the future. One way that He shares His message of hope is through the words of encouraging friends and family members.

Hope, like other human emotions, is contagious. If we associate with hope-filled, enthusiastic people, their enthusiasm will have a tendency to lift our spirits. But if we find ourselves spending too much time in the company of naysayers, pessimists, or cynics, our thoughts—like the naysayers'—will tend to be negative.

Are you a hopeful, optimistic Christian? And do you associate with like-minded people? If so, then you're availing yourself of a priceless gift: the gift of encouragement that is freely offered by fellow believers. But, if you find yourself focusing on the negative aspects of life, perhaps it is time to start searching for a few new friends.

As a faithful follower of the One from Galilee, you have every reason to be hopeful. So, if you have become discouraged with the direction of your day or your life, turn your thoughts and prayers to God—and associate with like-minded believers who do the same. And remember this: your Heavenly Father is a God of possibility, not negativity. He is your shepherd; He never leaves your side; and the ultimate victory will be His. So how, then, can you ever stay discouraged for long?

God's Word About . . . DISCOURAGEMENT

Have I not commanded you? Be strong and of good courage;
do not be afraid, nor be dismayed, for the Lord your God
is with you wherever you go.

JOSHUA 1:9 NKJV

And let us not grow weary while doing good,
for in due season we shall reap if we do not lose heart.

GALATIANS 6:9 NKJV

For consider Him who endured such hostility from sinners
against Himself, lest you become weary and
discouraged in your souls.

HEBREWS 12:3 NKJV

These things I have spoken to you, that in Me you
may have peace. In the world you will have tribulation;
but be of good cheer, I have overcome the world.

JOHN 16:33 NKJV

I was learning something important: we are most
vulnerable to the piercing winds of doubt when
we distance ourselves from the mission and fellowship to
which Christ has called us. Our night of discouragement
will seem endless and our task impossible,
unless we recognize that He stands in our midst.

JONI EARECKSON TADA

When we yield to discouragement, it is usually because
we give too much thought to the past or to the future.

ST. THÉRÈSE OF LISIEUX

You are justified in avoiding people who send you from
their presence with less hope and strength to cope with
life's problems than when you met them.

ELLA WHEELER WILCOX

Working in the vineyard, Working all the day,
Never be discouraged, Only watch and pray.

FANNY CROSBY

Additional Bible Readings

2 CORINTHIANS 4:8, 9; 2 CORINTHIANS 12:9, 10; HABAKKUK 3:17-19;

JEREMIAH 29:11; PSALM 27:14; ROMANS 8:37-39

DOUBT

Have you ever felt your faith in God slipping away? If so, you are not alone. Every life—including yours—is a series of successes and failures, celebrations and disappointments, joys and sorrows, hopes and doubts. Even the most faithful Christians are overcome by occasional bouts of fear and doubt, and so, too, will you.

Doubts come in several shapes and sizes: doubts about God, doubts about the future, and doubts about our own abilities, for starters. And what, precisely, does God's Word say in response to these doubts? The Bible is clear: when we are beset by doubts, of whatever kind, we must draw ourselves nearer to God through worship and through prayer. When we do so, God, the loving Father who has never left our sides, draws ever closer to us (James 4:8).

In the book of Matthew, we are told of a terrible storm that rose quickly on the Sea of Galilee while Jesus and His disciples were in a boat, far from shore. The disciples were filled with fear. Although they had witnessed many miracles firsthand, although they had walked with Jesus, and talked with Him, and seen His powers, they were still filled with doubts. The disciples cried out to their Master, and Christ responded,

"Why are you fearful, O you of little faith?" Then He arose and rebuked the winds and the sea, and there was a great calm. So

the men marveled, saying, "Who can this be, that even the winds and the sea obey Him?" Matthew 8:26, 27 NKJV

Sometimes, like Jesus' disciples, we feel threatened by the storms of life. Sometimes we may feel distant from God; sometimes we may question His power or His plans. During these moments, when we our hearts are flooded with uncertainty and doubt, we must remember that God is not simply near, He is here.

Will your faith be tested from time to time? Of course it will be. And will you have doubts about God's willingness to fulfill His promises? Perhaps you will. But even when you feel far removed from God, God never leaves your side, not even for an instant. He is always with you, always willing to calm the storms of life. When you sincerely seek His presence—and when you genuinely seek to establish a deeper, more meaningful relationship with His Son—God is prepared to touch your heart, to calm your fears, to answer your doubts, and to restore your soul.

So Jesus answered and said to them, "Have faith in God. For assuredly, I say to you, whoever says to this mountain, 'Be removed and be cast into the sea,' and does not doubt in his heart, but believes that those things he says will be done, he will have whatever he says. Therefore I say to you, whatever things you ask when you pray, believe that you receive them, and you will have them.

MARK 11:22-24 NKJV

So He said, "Come." And when Peter had come down out of the boat, he walked on the water to go to Jesus. But when he saw that the wind was boisterous, he was afraid; and beginning to sink he cried out, saying, "Lord, save me!" And immediately Jesus stretched out His hand and caught him, and said to him, "O you of little faith, why did you doubt?" And when they got into the boat, the wind ceased.

MATTHEW 14:29-32 NKJV

And He said to them, "Why are you troubled? And why do doubts arise in your hearts? Behold My hands and My feet, that it is I Myself. Handle Me and see, for a spirit does not have flesh and bones as you see I have." When He had said this, He showed them His hands and His feet.

LUKE 24:38-40 NKJV

More Thoughts About . . . DOUBT

Doubting may temporarily disturb,
but will not permanently destroy, your faith in Christ.

CHARLES SWINDOLL

Ignoring Him by neglecting prayer and
Bible reading will cause you to doubt.

ANNE GRAHAM LOTZ

There is a difference between doubt and unbelief.
Doubt is a matter of mind: we cannot understand what
God is doing or why He is doing it. Unbelief is a matter
of will: we refuse to believe God's Word and
obey what He tells us to do.

WARREN WIERSBE

Seldom do you enjoy the luxury of making decisions
that are based on enough evidence to absolutely silence
all skepticism.

BILL HYBELS

Additional Bible Readings

1 TIMOTHY 2:8; JOHN 20:29; HEBREWS 10:23; MATTHEW 12:38-40

FEELING UNFULFILLED

Everywhere we turn, or so it seems, the world promises fulfillment, contentment, and happiness. But the contentment that the world offers is fleeting and incomplete. Thankfully, the fulfillment that God offers is all encompassing and everlasting.

If you're feeling unfulfilled, and if you'd like a solution to that dilemma, try asking yourself two simple questions: 1. "Am I seeking fulfillment, first and foremost, through God, or am I seeking fulfillment through other means?" and 2. "Am I using the gifts and talents that God has given me, or am I trying to use talents that I wish He had given me?" These two questions can be simplified further: 1. "Am I genuinely placing God first in my life?" and 2. "Am I a beautiful square peg trying to squeeze myself into an ill-fitting round hole?"

PLACING GOD FIRST

God's Word instructs us to worship Him and only Him (Exodus 20:3), yet we are sorely tempted to do otherwise. We are tempted to seek fulfillment from worldly sources, and when we do so, we distance ourselves from God as we mistakenly worship things such as fame, fortune, popularity, or personal gratification. Inevitably, we find these pursuits unfulfilling.

The world makes promises that it simply cannot keep. The world promises pleasure and abundance, but genuine abundance is not a function of worldly possessions or personal gratification; genuine abundance is a function of our thoughts, our actions, and our relationship with God. The world's promises are incomplete and illusory; God's promises are unfailing.

We must build our lives on the firm foundation of God's promises—and we must place God first in our lives. Nothing less will suffice.

RECOGNIZING AND REFINING OUR TALENTS

Another source of distress stems from a common human failure: the failure to fully recognize and refine the talents that God has given us. Each of us possesses special abilities, gifted by God, that can be nurtured carefully or ignored totally. Our challenge, of course, is to use our talents to the greatest extent possible. But we are mightily tempted to do the opposite. Why? Because converting raw talent into polished skill usually requires perseverance, and lots of it. God's Word clearly instructs us to do the hard work of honing our talents for the glory of His kingdom (Matthew 25:18-30). When we do otherwise, we allow ourselves to drift aimlessly through life with our potential—and our hearts—unfulfilled.

Sometimes we take our talents for granted, and sometimes we ignore them altogether. Instead of using the gifts that God has given us, we seek to "fit in" with the crowd by settling for mediocrity or worse. But if we seek to be fulfilled, we must carefully consider the old saying: "What we're is God's gift to us; what we become is our gift to God." And we must act accordingly.

~

Sometimes, amid the inevitable hustle and bustle of life here on earth, we can forfeit—albeit temporarily—the joy of Christ as we wrestle with the challenges of daily living. Yet God's Word is clear: fulfillment through Christ is available to all who genuinely seek it and claim it. Count yourself among that number. Place God first, study His Word, seek His presence, and obey His commandments. Then, promise yourself that you will use God's gifts to the best of your abilities. When you do these things, you can then lay claim to the joy, the fulfillment, and the spiritual abundance that the Shepherd offers His sheep.

For I know the thoughts that I think toward you, says the Lord, thoughts of peace and not of evil, to give you a future and a hope.

—

JEREMIAH 29:11 NKJV

We all have different gifts, each of which came because of the grace God gave us. The person who has the gift of prophecy should use that gift in agreement with the faith. Anyone who has the gift of serving should serve. Anyone who has the gift of teaching should teach. Whoever has the gift of encouraging others should encourage. Whoever has the gift of giving to others should give freely. Anyone who has the gift of being a leader should try hard when he leads. Whoever has the gift of showing mercy to others should do so with joy.

ROMANS 12:6-8 NCV

Do not change yourselves to be like the people of this world, but be changed within by a new way of thinking. Then you will be able to decide what God wants for you; you will know what is good and pleasing to him and what is perfect. Because God has given me a special gift, I have something to say to everyone among you. Do not think you are better than you are. You must decide what you really are by the amount of faith God has given you.

ROMANS 12:2, 3 NCV

Until now you have not asked for anything in my name. Ask and you will receive, so that your joy will be the fullest possible joy.

JOHN 16:24 NCV

Find satisfaction in him who made you, and only then find satisfaction in yourself as part of his creation.

ST. AUGUSTINE

By trying to grab fulfillment everywhere,
we find it nowhere.

ELISABETH ELLIOT

Our sense of joy, satisfaction, and fulfillment in life increases, no matter what the circumstances,
if we are in the center of God's will.

BILLY GRAHAM

There's a unique sense of fulfillment that comes when we submit our gifts to God's use and ask him to energize them in a supernatural way—and then step back to watch what he does. It can be the difference between merely existing in black and white and living a life in full, brilliant color.

LEE STROBEL

Additional Bible Readings

JOHN 17:13; MATTHEW 5:6; PSALM 66:10–12; PSALM 90:14

HOPELESSNESS

On the darkest days of our lives, we may be confronted with an illusion that seems very real indeed: the illusion of hopelessness. Try though we might, we simply can't envision a solution to our problems—and we fall into the darkness of despair. During these times, we may question God: His love, His presence, even His very existence. Despite God's promises, despite Christ's love, and despite our many blessings, we may envision little or no hope for the future. These dark days are dangerous times for us and for our loved ones.

If you find yourself beset by feelings of hopelessness, take time to read the discussion about depression that appears earlier in this book. Then, take time to consider a simple, threefold prescription that serves as an antidote to despair. That prescription contains three simple elements: perspective, trust, and action.

PERSPECTIVE

When Old Man Trouble knocks on the door, it's easy to lose perspective—easy to assume that "all is lost,"—easy, but wrong. With God by your side and Jesus in your heart, all is never lost, and no earthly problem, no matter how big, is insurmountable.

If a temporary loss of perspective has left you worried, exhausted, or both, it's time to readjust your thought patterns.

Remember this: Exaggerated negative thoughts can be habit-forming and destructive. Thankfully, you need not fall prey to the habit of negative thinking. With practice, you can learn to focus, not upon the gloomier aspects of life, but upon God's priorities and your possibilities. When you do, you'll spend less time fretting about your challenges and more time praising God for His gifts.

FAITH

Jesus taught his disciples that if they had faith, they could do things that seemed impossible (Matthew 17:20). What was true for Christ's disciples is also true for you. When you place your faith, your trust, indeed your life in the hands of God, you'll be amazed at the marvelous things He can do with you and through you. Your challenge, then, is clear: You must take whatever measures are needed to strengthen your faith. Those measures include prayer, praise, worship, Bible study, and a regularly scheduled time of consultation with your Creator.

Can you place your future into the hands of a loving and all-knowing God? Can you live amid the uncertainties of today, knowing that God has dominion over all your tomorrows? Can you summon the faith to trust God in good times and hard times? If you can, you are wise and you are blessed.

ACTION

The willingness to take action—even if the outcome of that action is uncertain—is another way to combat hopelessness. When you decide to roll up your sleeves and begin solving your own problems, you'll feel empowered and you may see the first real glimmer of hope.

If you're waiting for someone else to solve your problems, or if you're waiting for God to patch things up by Himself, you may become impatient, despondent, or both. But when you stop waiting and start working, God has a way of pitching in and finishing the job. The advice of American publisher Cyrus Curtis still rings true: "Believe in the Lord and he will do half the work—the last half."

With God by your side, you need never lose hope. So today and every day, ask God for these things: clear perspective, mountain-moving faith, and the courage to do what needs doing. After all, no problem is too big for God—not even yours.

Rejoicing in hope,

patient in tribulation,

continuing steadfastly in prayer.

—

ROMANS 12:12

Therefore we do not lose heart.
Even though our outward man is perishing,
yet the inward man is being renewed day by day.

2 CORINTHIANS 4:16 NKJV

Let us hold fast the confession of our hope without wavering,
for He who promised is faithful.

HEBREWS 10:23 NKJV

Be of good courage, and He shall strengthen your heart,
all you who hope in the Lord.

PSALM 31:24 NKJV

Now may the God of hope fill you with all joy and
peace in believing, that you may abound in hope by
the power of the Holy Spirit.

ROMANS 15:13 NKJV

When you and I are related to Jesus Christ, our strength and wisdom and peace and joy and love and hope may run out, but His life rushes in to keep us filled to the brim. We are showered with blessings, not because of anything we have or have not done, but simply because of Him.

ANNE GRAHAM LOTZ

The essence of optimism is that it takes no account of the present, but it is a source of inspiration, of vitality, and of hope. Where others have resigned, it enables a man to hold his head high, to claim the future for himself, and not abandon it to his enemy.

DIETRICH BONHOEFFER

In those desperate times when we feel like we don't have an ounce of strength, He will gently pick up our heads so that our eyes can behold something—something that will keep His hope alive in us.

KATHY TROCCOLI

Christ has turned all our sunsets into dawn.

ST. CLEMENT OF ALEXANDRIA

Additional Bible Readings

HEBREWS 6:19; LAMENTATIONS 3:25, 26; PROVERBS 13:12; PSALM 71:5

PERFECTIONISM

Expectations, expectations, expectations! As members-in-good-standing of the 21st century, we know all too well that the demands of everyday living can be high, and expectations of society can be even higher. The media delivers an endless stream of messages telling us how to look, how to behave, how to eat, and how to dress. The media's expectations are impossible to meet—God's are not. God doesn't expect us to be perfect . . . and neither, for that matter, should we.

The difference between perfectionism and realistic expectations is the difference between a life of frustration and a life of contentment. Only one earthly being ever lived a perfect lfe, and He was the Son of God. The rest of us have fallen short of God's standard and need to be accepting of our own limitations as well as the limitations of others.

If you find yourself frustrated by the unrealistic demands of others (or by unrealistic pressures of the self-imposed variety) it's time to ask yourself whom you're trying to impress, and why. If you're trying to impress your friends, or if you're trying to imitate the appearance of some rail-thin Hollywood celebrity or chisled male model, it's time to reconsider your priorities. Here's a brief review:

Priority One: Your first responsibility is to the Heavenly Father who created you and to His only begotten Son, the One who offers you eternal salvation.

Priority Two: Whether you realize it or not, you bear a responsibility to yourself—a responsibility to respect yourself and to honor the unique person whom God created. That means honoring yourself despite your imperfections.

Priority Three: You also owe debts of gratitude to friends and family members; but you do not owe them perfection; God doesn't expect perfection—and neither should they.

As you consider these three priorities, you'll quickly notice that meeting society's unrealistic expectations is not on the list, nor should it be. So the next time you feel overwhelmed by feelings that you simply don't measure up to the sky-high standards of our modern world, remember this: when you accepted Christ as your Savior, God accepted you for all eternity. Now, it's your turn to accept yourself. When you do, you'll feel a tremendous weight being lifted from your shoulders. After all, pleasing God is simply a matter of obeying His commandments and accepting His Son. But as for pleasing everybody else? That's impossible!

God began doing a good work in you, and I am sure he will continue it until it is finished when Jesus Christ comes again.

PHILIPPIANS 1:6 NCV

Your beliefs about these things should be kept secret between you and God. People are happy if they can do what they think is right without feeling guilty.

ROMANS 14:22 NCV

For You have made him a little lower than the angels, And You have crowned him with glory and honor.

PSALM 8:5 NKJV

The work of righteousness will be peace, And the effect of righteousness, quietness and assurance forever.

ISAIAH 32:17 NKJV

God is so inconceivably good. He's not looking
for perfection. He already saw it in Christ.
He's looking for affection.

BETH MOORE

The happiest people in the world are not those who have
no problems, but the people who have learned to live
with those things that are less than perfect.

JAMES DOBSON

What makes a Christian a Christian is not perfection
but forgiveness.

MAX LUCADO

If you try to be everything to everybody,
you will end up being nothing to anybody.

VANCE HAVNER

Additional Bible Readings

PSALM 71:5; PHILIPPIANS 4:11-13

PRIDE

Dietrich Bonhoeffer observed, "It is very easy to overestimate the importance of our own achievements in comparison with what we owe others." How true. Even those of us who consider ourselves "self-made" men and women are deeply indebted to more people than we can count. Our first and greatest indebtedness, of course, is to God and to His only begotten Son. But we are also indebted to ancestors, parents, teachers, friends, spouses, family members, coworkers, fellow believers…and the list goes on.

With so many people who rightfully deserve to share the credit for our successes, how can we gloat? The answer, of course, is that when we are honest with ourselves, we should never gloat about our accomplishments.

Proverbs 16:18 warns us that "Pride goes before destruction…" (NKJV). And 1 Peter 5:5 teaches us that "God is against the proud, but he gives grace to the humble" (NCV). The message is straightforward: if we trust God's Word, we must clearly understand the dangers of pride. But sometimes, our feelings of pride are so subtle that we fail to recognize them for what they are, mistaking unhealthy pride for "self-confidence" or "self-assurance."

Self-confidence and self-assurance are wonderful traits as long as we keep them in check. But if we allow our feelings of self-importance to obscure our dependence upon God, then we invite His displeasure.

The next time you experience a noteworthy success, remember this: You are entitled to take pride in your accomplishments, but not too much pride. So instead of puffing out your chest and saying, "Look at me!", give credit where credit is due, starting with God. And remember, too, that there is no such thing as a self-made man or woman.

All of us are made by God—and He deserves the glory, not us.

IT WAS PRIDE THAT CHANGED ANGELS INTO DEVILS; IT IS HUMILITY THAT MAKES MEN AS ANGELS.

—

ST. AUGUSTINE

Pride goes before destruction, and a haughty spirit before a fall.

PROVERBS 16:18 NKJV

*Therefore humble yourselves under the mighty hand of God,
that He may exalt you in due time.*

1 PETER 5:6 NKJV

*Respecting the Lord and not being proud will bring you wealth,
honor, and life.*

PROVERBS 22:4 NCV

*The greatest among you must be a servant.
But those who exalt themselves will be humbled, and
those who humble themselves will be exalted.*

MATTHEW 23:11, 12 NKJV

The Lord sends no one away empty except
those who are full of themselves.

D. L. MOODY

Pride has a devilish quality that keeps us from sensing
our need for God's grace.

JIM CYMBALA

The proud man counts his newspaper clippings,
the humble man his blessings.

FULTON J. SHEEN

God wants you to know Him: He wants to give you
Himself.... If you really get into any kind of touch with
Him you will, in fact, be humble, delightedly humble,
feeling the infinite relief of having for once got rid of all
the silly nonsense about you own dignity which has made
you restless and unhappy all your life.

C. S. LEWIS

Additional Bible Readings

JAMES 4:10; PHILIPPIANS 2:3; PROVERBS 18:12; ROMANS 12:3

QUESTIONING, UNCERTAINTY, AND TRUST

As mortal beings with limited understanding, we simply cannot understand the workings of God. Were we to arrange the world according to our own wishes, bad things would never happen to good people, and the stories of our lives would always end "happily ever after." But the world doesn't work that way, and at times, we simply can't understand why.

Sometimes, people get sick; sometimes, people are hurt; sometimes, tragedies befall innocent bystanders. And, when bad things happen to innocent people, we have plenty of questions and very few answers.

God does not explain Himself in ways that we humans might prefer. When innocent people are hurt, we may find ourselves questioning God because we can't understand exactly what He's doing, or why. Why are righteous people allowed to feel pain and good people allowed to die? We simply can't understand why.

Some day, we will understand God's plans with clarity. The words of 1 Corinthians 13:12 make this promise: "For now we see in a mirror, dimly, but then face to face. Now I know in part, but then I shall know just as I also am known" (NKJV). So, we can be comforted in the knowledge that even though our questions may go unanswered today, we will gain complete understanding in heaven. Until that glorious day, we must trust that the Shepherd will care for His sheep.

You are precious in the eyes of God. You are His priceless creation, made in His image, and protected by Him. God watches over every step you make and every breath you take, so you need never be afraid, and you need never lose hope. Yet sometimes, your faith will be tested—on occasion, you will confront circumstances that trouble you to the very core of your soul. When you are afraid, trust in God. When you are worried, turn your concerns over to Him. When you are anxious, be still and listen for the quiet assurance of God's promises. When you have questions that you simply cannot answer, trust your Heavenly Father. And then, place your life in His hands. He is your shepherd today and throughout eternity. Trust the Shepherd.

God's Word About . . . QUESTIONING, UNCERTAINTY, AND TRUST

Trust the Lord with all your heart, and don't depend on your own understanding.

PROVERBS 3:5 NCV

Wisdom is the principal thing; therefore get wisdom. And in all your getting, get understanding.

PROVERBS 4:7 NKJV

And he said: "The Lord is my rock and my fortress and my deliverer; the God of my strength, in whom I will trust."

2 SAMUEL 22:2, 3 NKJV

Jesus said, "Don't let your hearts be troubled. Trust in God, and trust in me."

JOHN 14:1 NCV

More Thoughts About . . . QUESTIONING, UNCERTAINTY, AND TRUST

A prudent question is one-half of wisdom.

FRANCIS BACON

O Lord, thank You that Your side of the embroidery of our life is always perfect. That is such a comfort when our side is sometimes so mixed up.

CORRIE TEN BOOM

Since we can't understand that God does, we must trust everything that God is.

MARIE T. FREEMAN

We shall steer safely through every storm, as long as our heart is right, our intention fervent, our courage steadfast, and our trust fixed in God.

ST. FRANCIS OF SALES

Accepting the mystery of what we cannot know will lead us to the heart of God where we trade our craving for explanation for a simple willingness to trust.

PAULA RINEHART

Additional Bible Readings

2 CORINTHIANS 5:7; PSALM 18:2; PSALM 56:3; DEUTERONOMY 31:8

SELF-ESTEEM AND SELF-IMAGE

When God made you, he equipped you with an array of talents and abilities that are uniquely yours. It's up to you to discover those talents and to use them, but sometimes the world will encourage you to do otherwise. At times, society will attempt to cubbyhole you, to standardize you, and to make you fit into particular, preformed mold. Perhaps God has other plans.

Sometimes, because you're an imperfect human being, you may become so wrapped up in meeting society's expectations that you fail to focus on God's expectations. To do so is a mistake of major proportions—don't make it. Instead, seek God's guidance as you focus your energies on becoming the best "you" that you can possibly be. And when it comes to matters of self-esteem and self-image, seek approval not from your peers, but from your God.

Millions of words have been written about various ways to improve self-image and increase self-esteem. Yet, maintaining a healthy self-image is, to a surprising extent, a matter of doing three things: 1.Obeying God 2. Thinking healthy thoughts 3. Finding a purpose for your life that pleases your Creator and yourself. The following common-sense, Biblically-based tips can help you build the kind of self-image—and the kind of life—that both you and God can be proud of:

1. Do the right thing: If you're misbehaving, how can you possibly hope to feel good about yourself? (Romans 14:12)

2. Watch what you think: If your inner voice is, in reality, your inner critic, you need to tone down the criticism now. And while you're at it, train yourself to begin thinking thoughts that are more rational, more accepting, and less judgmental. (Philippians 4:8)

3. Spend time with boosters, not critics: Are your friends putting you down? If so, find new friends. (Hebrews 3:13)

4. Don't be a perfectionist: Strive for excellence, but never confuse it with perfection. (Ecclesiastes 11:4, 6)

5. Find something that you're passionate about: Become so busy following your passion that you forget to worry about your self-esteem. (Colossians 3:23)

6. If you're addicted to something unhealthy, stop; if you can't stop, get help: Addictions, of whatever type, create havoc in your life. And disorder. And grief. And low self esteem. (Exodus 20:3)

7. Find a purpose for your life that is larger than you are: When you're dedicated to something or someone besides yourself, you blossom. (Ephesians 6:7)

8. Don't worry too much about self-esteem: Instead, worry more about living a life that is pleasing to God. Learn to think optimistically. Find a worthy purpose. Find people to love and people to serve. When you do, your self-esteem will, on most days, take care of itself. (Philippians 2:4)

This is why I remind you to keep using the gift
God gave you when I laid my hands on you.
Now let it grow, as a small flame grows into a fire.

2 TIMOTHY 1:6 NCV

For we are His workmanship, created in Christ Jesus
for good works, which God prepared beforehand
that we should walk in them.

EPHESIANS 2:10 NKJV

You made my whole being; you formed me in my mother's body.
I praise you because you made me in an amazing and wonderful
way. What you have done is wonderful. I know this very well.
You saw my bones being formed as I took shape in my mother's
body. When I was put together there, you saw my body
as it was formed. All the days planned for me
were written in your book before I was one day old.

PSALM 139:13-16 NCV

God did not give us a spirit that makes us afraid but
a spirit of power and love and self-control.

2 TIMOTHY 1:7 NCV

Believe in yourself. Have faith in your abilities.
Without a humble but reasonable confidence in
your own powers, you can't be successful or happy.

NORMAN VINCENT PEALE

Being loved by Him whose opinion matters most gives us
the security to risk loving, too—even loving ourselves.

GLORIA GAITHER

As you and I lay up for ourselves living, lasting treasures in
Heaven, we come to the awesome conclusion
that we ourselves are His treasure!

ANNE GRAHAM LOTZ

You are valuable just because you exist.
Not because of what you do or what you have done,
but simply because you are.

MAX LUCADO

Perhaps I am stronger than I think.

THOMAS MERTON

Additional Bible Readings

1 PETER 2:9; JOHN 3:16; ROMANS 8:31; ROMANS 8:35-39

TEMPTATION

Because our world is filled with temptations, we confront them at every turn. Some of these temptations are small—eating a second piece of chocolate cake, for example. Too much cake may cause us to defile, at least in a modest way, the bodily temple that God has entrusted to our care. But two pieces of cake will not bring us to our knees. Other temptations, however, are not so harmless.

The devil, it seems, is working overtime these days, and causing heartache in more places and in more ways than ever before. We, as Christians, must remain vigilant. Not only must we resist Satan when he confronts us, but we must also avoid those places where Satan can most easily tempt us. And, if we are to avoid the unending temptations of this world, we must arm ourselves with the Word of God.

In a letter to believers, Peter offered a stern warning: "Be sober, be vigilant; because your adversary the devil walks about like a roaring lion, seeking whom he may devour." (1 Peter 5:8 NKJV). What was true in New Testament times is equally true in our own. Satan tempts his prey and then devours them. And in these dangerous times, the tools that Satan uses to destroy his prey are more numerous than ever before.

As believing Christians, we must beware. And, if we seek righteousness in our own lives, we must earnestly wrap ourselves in the protection of God's Holy Word. After fasting forty days and nights in the desert, Jesus Himself was tempted by Satan. Christ used scripture to rebuke the devil. (Matthew 4:1-11) We must do likewise. The Holy Bible provides us with a perfect blueprint for righteous living. If we consult that blueprint daily and follow it carefully, we build our lives according to God's plan. And when we do, we are secure.

WE CAN'T STOP THE ADVERSARY FROM WHISPERING IN OUR EARS, BUT WE CAN REFUSE TO LISTEN, AND WE CAN DEFINITELY REFUSE TO RESPOND.

—

LIZ CURTIS HIGGS

No temptation has overtaken you except such as is common to man; but God is faithful, who will not allow you to be tempted beyond what you are able, but with the temptation will also make the way of escape, that you may be able to bear it.

1 CORINTHIANS 10:13 NKJV

But I discipline my body and bring it into subjection, lest, when I have preached to others, I myself should become disqualified.

1 CORINTHIANS 9:27 NKJV

Blessed is the man who endures temptation; for when he has been approved, he will receive the crown of life which the Lord has promised to those who love Him.

JAMES 1:12 NKJV

The Lord knows how to deliver the godly out of temptations.

2 PETER 2:9 NKJV

Our Lord has given us an example of how to overcome
the devil's temptations. When he was tempted in
the wilderness, He defeated Satan every time by
the use of the Bible.

BILLY GRAHAM

The heart of man is revealed in temptation.
Man knows his sin, which without temptation he could
never have known, for it is in temptation man knows on
what he has set his heart. The coming to light of sin is
the work of the accuser, who thereby thinks to have won
the victory. But, it is sin that has become manifest that can
be known, and therefore forgiven. Thus, the manifestation
of sin belongs to the salvation plan of God with man,
and Satan must serve this plan.

DIETRICH BONHOEFFER

The higher the hill, the stronger the wind:
so the loftier the life, the stronger the enemy's temptations.

JOHN WYCLIFFE

Additional Bible Readings

MATTHEW 4:10; MATTHEW 26:41; PROVERBS 1:10; ROMANS 8:6

WORRY

Because we have the ability to think, we also have the ability to worry. From time to time, all of us are plagued by occasional periods of discouragement and doubt. Even though we may believe sincerely in God's love and protection, we may find ourselves fretting over the countless obligations and details of everyday life.

Because of His humanity, Jesus understood the inevitability of worry. And he addressed the topic clearly and forcefully in the 6th chapter of Matthew:

Therefore I say to you, do not worry about your life, what you will eat or what you will drink; nor about your body, what you will put on. Is not life more than food and the body more than clothing? Look at the birds of the air, for they neither sow nor reap nor gather into barns; yet your heavenly Father feeds them. Are you not of more value than they? Which of you by worrying can add one cubit to his stature? . . . Therefore do not worry about tomorrow, for tomorrow will worry about its own things. Sufficient for the day is its own trouble. v. 25-27, 34

More often than not, our worries stem from an inability to focus and to trust. We fail to focus on a priceless gift from God: the profound, precious, present moment. Instead of thanking God for the blessings of this day, we choose to fret about two more ominous days: yesterday and tomorrow. We stew about the unfairness of the past, or we agonize about the uncertainty of the future. Such thinking stirs up negative feelings that prepare our hearts and minds for an equally destructive emotion: fear.

Our fears are rooted in a failure to trust. Instead of trusting God's plans for our lives, we fix our minds on countless troubles that might come to pass (but seldom do). A better strategy, of course, is to take God at His word by trusting His promises. Our Lord has promised that He will care for our needs—needs, by the way, that He understands far more completely than we do. God's Word is unambiguous; so, too, should be our trust in Him.

In Matthew 6, Jesus instructs us to live in day-tight compartments. He reminds us that each day has enough worries of its own without the added weight of yesterday's regrets or tomorrow's fears. Perhaps you feel disturbed by the past or threatened by the future. Perhaps you are concerned about your relationships, your health, your career, or your finances. Or perhaps you are simply a "worrier" by nature. If so, make Matthew 6 a regular part of your daily Bible reading. This beautiful passage will remind you that God still sits in His heaven and you are His beloved child. Then, perhaps, you will worry less and trust God more. And that's as it should be because God is trustworthy…and you are protected.

Come to Me, all you who labor and are heavy laden,
and I will give you rest. Take My yoke upon you and learn
from Me, for I am gentle and lowly in heart, and you will find
rest for your souls. For My yoke is easy and My burden is light.

MATTHEW 11:28-30 NKJV

Let not your heart be troubled; you believe in God,
believe also in Me.

JOHN 14:1 NKJV

Be anxious for nothing, but in everything by prayer
and supplication, with thanksgiving,
let your requests be made known to God.

PHILIPPIANS 4:6 NKJV

Give your worries to the Lord, and he will take care of you.
He will never let good people down.

PSALM 55:22 NCV

Worry is a cycle of inefficient thoughts whirling around a center of fear.

CORRIE TEN BOOM

We hope vaguely, but we dread precisely.

PAUL VALÉRY

Much that worries us beforehand can, quite unexpectedly, have a happy and simple solution. Worries just don't matter. Things really are in a better hand than ours.

DIETRICH BONHOEFFER

The secret of Christian quietness is not indifference, but the knowledge that God is my Father, He loves me, and that I shall never think of anything that He will forget. Then, worry becomes an impossibility.

OSWALD CHAMBERS

Additional Bible Readings

1 PETER 5:6, 7; 2 SAMUEL 22:2, 3; PROVERBS 3:5, 6; PSALM 56:11;

PSALM 84:11, 12; PSALM 118:8, 9

PART II

OUR RELATIONSHIPS

Our relationships help define who we are today and who we will become tomorrow. Our relationships have the power to enrich us or restrict us. And the quality of our relationships depends, in large part, on the person who faces you each time you gaze into the mirror.

In Part II of God's Survival Guide, we consider ways to understand our relationships . . . and ways to improve them.

ABUSIVE RELATIONSHIPS

In a perfect world inhabited by perfect people, all our relationships would be uplifting, enlightening, encouraging, and loving. But this world is populated by decidedly imperfect people, and as a result, our relationships are equally imperfect. On occasion, relationships become abusive, and when they do, it's time for the aggrieved party to take firm, rational, and immediate action.

If you're involved in a troubling or abusive relationship, here are some "do's and don'ts":

1. Don't think of yourself as a victim: Think of yourself as a person who needs to take action now—and think of yourself as a person who can! (James 1:22)

2. Do consider your options: And remember this: If you think you don't have any options, you're not thinking clearly enough. (Luke 18:27)

3. Do seek help: Whether you realize it or not, lots of folks want to help you; let them. (Proverbs 11:25)

4. Don't try to "change" the other person: Trying to "reform" other people is usually futile; other people must reform themselves—and hopefully, with God's help, they will do so—but you cannot force them to do so. (Psalm 118: 8, 9)

5. Do insist upon logical consequences: If the other person misbehaves—or worse—allow him or her to learn from the consequences of that misbehavior (in other words, don't be an "enabler"). (Hebrews 12:5, 6)

6. Don't give up hope: Other people have experienced the same kind of hard times you may be experiencing now. They made it, and so can you. (Psalm 146:5)

7. Do make your personal safety the highest priority: If you're in an explosive relationship, do the wise thing—think "safety first": safety for yourself and, if you're a parent, safety for your children. (Proverbs 3:18)

A destructive relationship seldom starts out that way—in the beginning, the relationship may seem ideal, or nearly so. But over time, as the relationship gradually begins to deteriorate, small problems evolve into big troubles. So, if you find yourself in a relationship that is harmful to your health, your safety, or your sanity, don't be satisfied with the status quo. Pray for strength; pray for wisdom; pray for courage; and then, get busy creating a better world for you and yours.

Make no friendship with an angry man.

PROVERBS 22:24 NKJV

*Nevertheless God, who comforts the downcast,
comforted us . . . .*

2 CORINTHIANS 7:6 NKJV

*This is my comfort in my affliction,
For Your word has given me life.*

PSALM 119:50 NKJV

*And the Lord, He is the one who goes before you.
He will be with you,
He will not leave you nor forsake you;
do not fear nor be dismayed.*

DEUTERONOMY 31:8 NKJV

The knowledge that we are never alone calms
the troubled sea of our lives and speaks peace to our souls.

A.W. TOZER

Suffering may be someone's fault or it may not be
anyone's fault. But if given to God, our suffering becomes
an opportunity to experience the power of God at work
in our lives and to give glory to Him.

ANNE GRAHAM LOTZ

God whispers to us in our pleasures,
speaks in our conscience, but shouts in our pain.

C. S. LEWIS

By ourselves we are not capable of suffering bravely,
but the Lord possesses all the strength we lack and
will demonstrate His power when we undergo persecution.

CORRIE TEN BOOM

Additional Bible Readings

PSALM 27:10; PSALM 46; PSALM 88; PSALM 107:20; PSALM 130:1, 2

AGING PARENTS

If you're responsible, either directly or indirectly, for the care of aging parents, you already know that it's challenging job at times. But you also know that caring for your loved ones is not simply a duty; it is also a responsibility and a privilege.

Caring for an elderly adult requires a mixture of diplomacy, patience, insight, perseverance, gentleness, strength, compassion, wisdom, empathy, and, most of all, an endless supply of love. Because every situation is different, easy solutions can be elusive, but the following strategies can help:

1. Avoid anger: Of course it's easy to become frustrated when your aging parents don't behave themselves, but your anger isn't likely to improve their misbehavior. (1 Peter 2:1)

2. Practice the Golden Rule: Treat them in the same way you would want your children to treat you. (Matthew 7:12)

3. Pray About It: God has answers, and God answers prayer . . . so pray! (James 5:16)

4. Talk to the Experts: Experienced experts may not have all of the answers, but at least they'll know most of the questions! So ask, listen, and learn. (Proverbs 4:7)

5. Take an Active Role: If you don't, who will? Or should? (James 1:22)

6. Take Care of Yourself: Once again: If you don't, who will? Or should? (1 Corinthians 10:31)

7. Glorify God by Honoring Them: God wants you to honor your parents. Honor Him by honoring them. (Exodus 20:12)

Sometimes, the job of caring for aging parents may seem to be a thankless task, but it is not. Even if your parents don't fully appreciate your sacrifices, God does. And of this you may be certain: The Lord will find surprising ways to reward your faithfulness . . . now and in heaven.

Old people are proud of their grandchildren,
and children are proud of their parents.

PROVERBS 17:6 NCV

Listen to your father who begot you, and do not despise
your mother when she is old. The father of the righteous
will greatly rejoice, and he who begets a wise child will delight
in him. Let your father and your mother be glad,
and let her who bore you rejoice.

PROVERBS 23:22, 24, 25 NKJV

Honor your father and your mother, as the Lord your God
has commanded you, that your days may be long,
and that it may be well with you in the land
which the Lord your God is giving you.

DEUTERONOMY 5:16 NKJV

In the same way, younger people should be willing to be
under older people. And all of you should be very humble
with each other. "God is against the proud,
but he gives grace to the humble."

1 PETER 5:5 NCV

Spend time with your parents.
They're not around forever.

HUGH O'BRIEN

There is no friendship, no love,
like that of the parent for the child.

HENRY WARD BEECHER

Grow old along with me!
The best is yet to be,
The last of life, for which the first was made....

ROBERT BROWNING

You can only perceive real beauty in
a person as they get older.

ANOUK AIMEE

Additional Bible Readings

PSALM 37:25; PSALM 92:12-14; RUTH 1:16, 17; RUTH 3:10, 11

BEING SINGLE AND DATING

If you're officially "single and dating", you know from firsthand experience that dating isn't easy! Perhaps you've never been married. Or perhaps you've been "reintroduced" to the dating game after years of matrimony. In either case, you'll probably agree that finding the right person can be, at times, an exercise in "trial and error"—with a decided emphasis on "error." So, if you've found "Mr. or Miss Right", thank the Good Lord for your good fortune. But, you're still looking, here are some things to consider:

1. Place God first in every aspect of your life, including your dating life: He deserves first place, and any relationship that doesn't put Him there is the wrong relationship for you. (Exodus 20:3)

2. Be contented where you are, even if it's not exactly where you want to end up: Think about it like this: maybe God has somebody waiting in the wings. And remember that God's timing is always best. (Philippians 4:11, 12)

3. Be choosy: Don't "settle" for second-class treatment— you deserve someone who values you as a person . . . and shows it. (Psalm 40:1)

4. If you want to meet new people, go to the places where you are likely to bump into the kind of people you want to meet: you probably won't find the right kind of person in the wrong kind of place. (1 Corinthians 15:33)

5. Look beyond appearances: Judging other people solely by appearances is tempting, but it's foolish, shortsighted, immature, and ultimately destructive. So don't do it. (Proverbs 16:22)

6. Trust God: Your dating life, like every other aspect of your life, should glorify God; pray for His guidance, and follow it. (Proverbs 3:5, 6)

Don't kid yourself: being single and dating isn't all "fun and games." Dating can be stressful, very stressful. And remember that the choices you make in the dating world can have a profound impact on every other aspect of your life. So choose carefully and prayerfully.

You shall love the Lord your God with all your heart,
with all your soul, and with all your strength.

DEUTERONOMY 6:5 NKJV

Do not be unequally yoked together with unbelievers.
For what fellowship has righteousness with lawlessness?
And what communion has light with darkness?

2 CORINTHIANS 6:14 NKJV

Wisdom is the principal thing; therefore get wisdom.
And in all your getting, get understanding.

PROVERBS 4:7 NKJV

Depend on the Lord in whatever you do,
and your plans will succeed.

PROVERBS 16:3 NCV

Line by line, moment by moment, special times are
etched into our memories in the permanent ink of
everlasting love in our relationships.

GLORIA GAITHER

If God has you in the palm of his hand and your real life is
secure in him, then you can venture forth—
into the places and relationships, the challenges,
the very heart of the storm—and you will be safe there.

PAULA RINEHART

You have been made by God, for God, and apart from
Him there will always be emptiness in your soul.

ANGELA THOMAS

Beware that you are not swallowed up in books!
An ounce of love is worth a pound of knowledge.

JOHN WESLEY

Additional Bible Readings

1 PETER 1:22; 1 PETER 4:8; JOHN 13:34; ROMANS 8:28

CHALLENGES WITH CHILDREN:

THE DIFFICULTIES OF BEING A RESPONSIBLE PARENT

Every child is different, but every child is similar in this respect: he or she is a priceless gift from the Father above. And, with the Father's gift comes immense responsibilities for moms and dads alike.

Even on those difficult days when the house is in an uproar, the laundry is piled high, and the bills are piled even higher, wise parents never forget their overriding goal: shaping young minds and hearts. The very best parents shape those minds with love, with discipline, and with God.

Our children are our most precious resource. May we, as responsible Christians and dedicated parents, pray for our children here at home and for children around the world. Every child is God's child. May we, as loving and godly parents, behave—and teach—accordingly. The following Biblically-based tips can help:

1. "And the greatest of these is love . . ." When it comes to raising our kids, 1 Corinthians 13:13 certainly applies: The "greatest of these" is, indeed, love. Every child deserves to grow up in a safe, loving, God-fearing home, and if you're a parent, it's up to you to make certain that your home fits that description.

2. Teach by example: Parental pronouncements are easy to make but much harder to live by. As a parent, you are not just a role model; you are *the* role model. Behave accordingly. (Titus 2:7)

3. Safety first: As a responsible parent, it's up to you to be your family's safety expert. Impulsive kids, left to their own devices, tend to get themselves into dangerous situations; responsible adults, however, don't leave kids to their own devices. (Proverbs 27:12)

4. Allow your child to experience logical consequences: The world won't protect your child from the consequences of misbehavior, and neither should you. As a parent, your job is to ensure that the consequences of your child's actions are logical, measured, appropriate, and thoroughly understood by your youngster. (Hebrews 12:5, 6)

5. Ask lots of questions: When questions can be answered with a simple "yes" or "no," youngsters will tend to answer accordingly; a better strategy is to ask questions that require a more thoughtful response. Such questions might begin with: "How do you feel about…" or "What do you think about…". (James 1:19)

6. Watch and listen: Listen with your ears, your eyes, and your heart. And remember: wise parents pay careful attention to the things their children *don't* say. (Proverbs 1:5)

7. Share your faith: You need not have attended seminary to have worthwhile opinions about your faith. Express those opinions, especially to your children. Your kids need to know where you stand. (Joshua 24:15)

Train up a child in the way he should go,
And when he is old he will not depart from it.

PROVERBS 22:6 NKJV

Children, obey your parents in the Lord,
for this is right. "Honor your father and mother,"
which is the first commandment with promise:
"that it may be well with you and you may live long on
the earth." And you, fathers, do not provoke
your children to wrath, but bring them up in
the training and admonition of the Lord.

EPHESIANS 6:1-4 NKJV

Behold, children are a heritage from the Lord,
The fruit of the womb is a reward. Like arrows in the hand of
a warrior, So are the children of one's youth. Happy is the man
who has his quiver full of them; They shall not be ashamed,
But shall speak with their enemies in the gate.

PSALM 127:3-5 NKJV

Children's children are the crown of old men,
And the glory of children is their father.

PROVERBS 17:6 NKJV

When a child is convinced he is greatly loved and
respected by his parents, he is inclined to accept
his own worth as a person.

JAMES DOBSON

Parents need to listen and be patient as their children talk
to them. A listening ear and a loving ear
always go together.

WARREN WIERSBE

Father was the old-fashioned sort who believed
that the authority in the home belonged to parents and
not to the children.

VANCE HAVNER

There is nothing more special, more precious than
time that a parent spends struggling and pondering
with God on behalf of a child.

MAX LUCADO

Kids aren't looking for perfect parents, but
they are looking for honest and growing ones.

HOWARD HENDRICKS

Additional Bible Readings

MALACHI 4:6; DEUTERONOMY 6:5-9; PROVERBS 29:15-17; PROVERBS 23:24;

ISAIAH 54:13; HOSEA 14:4

DEALING WITH DIFFICULT PEOPLE

All of us can be grumpy, hardheaded, and difficult to deal with at times. And all of us, from time to time, encounter folks who behave in the same way, or worse. If you have occasion to deal with difficult people (and you will), the following tips should help:

1. Do Make Sure That You're Not the One Being Difficult: Perhaps the problems that concern you have their origin, at least partially, within your own heart. If so, fix yourself first. (Philippians 2:3)

2. Don't Try to Change the Other Person: Unless the person you're trying to change is a young child, and unless you are that child's parent or guardian, don't try to change him or her. Why? Because teenagers and adults change when they want to, not when you want them to. (Proverbs 10:14)

3. Don't Lecture: Lectures inevitably devolve into nagging; nagging creates animosity, not lasting change. Since nagging usually creates more problems than it solves, save your breath. (Proverbs 15:1)

4. Do Insist Upon Logical Consequences to Irresponsible Behavior: When you protect other people from the consequences of their misbehavior, you're doing those folks a profound disservice. Most people don't learn new behaviors until the old behaviors stop working, so don't be an enabler. (Hebrews 12:5, 6)

5. Don't Allow Yourself to Become Caught Up in the Other Person's Emotional Outbursts: If someone is ranting, raving, or worse, you have the right to get up and leave. Remember: Emotions are highly contagious, so if the other person is angry, you will soon become angry, too. Instead of adding your own emotional energy to the outburst, you should make the conscious effort to remain calm—and part of remaining calm may be leaving the scene of the argument. (Proverbs 22:24, 25)

6. Do Stand Up for Yourself: If you're being mistreated, either physically, emotionally, or professionally, it's time to start taking care of yourself. But remember that standing up for yourself doesn't require an angry outburst on your part; you can (and probably should) stand up for yourself in a calm, mature, resolute manner. And you should do so sooner rather than later. (Psalm 27:1)

7. Do Forgive: If you can't find it in your heart to forgive those who have hurt you, you're hurting yourself more than you're hurting anyone else. But remember: forgiveness should not be confused with enabling. Even after you've forgiven the difficult person in your life, you are not compelled to accept continued mistreatment from him or her. (Matthew 6:14, 15)

8. Do Learn to Laugh at the Absurdities of Life: Life has a lighter side—look for it, especially when times are tough. Laughter is medicine for the soul, so take your medicine early and often. (Proverbs 17:22)

9. Do Accept Personal Responsibility for Making Your Own Corner of the World Peaceful, Productive, Purposeful, and Palatable: If your world is a little crazy, perhaps it's time to consult the man or woman you see in the mirror. With God's help, you can discover a peace that passes understanding (Philippians 4:7, 8). And if you genuinely work to bring peace into your own life (and into the lives of your loved ones) you will be rewarded. (1 Corinthians 3:8, 13)

No one
CAN DRIVE US CRAZY
UNLESS
WE GIVE THEM
THE KEYS.

—

DOUG HORTON

But I say to you who hear: Love your enemies,
do good to those who hate you, bless those who curse you,
and pray for those who spitefully use you. To him who strikes
you on the one cheek, offer the other also. And from him who
takes away your cloak, do not withhold your tunic either.
Give to everyone who asks of you. And from him who
takes away your goods do not ask them back. And just as
you want men to do to you, you also do to them likewise.

LUKE 6:27-31 NKJV

This is My commandment, that you love one another as
I have loved you. Greater love has no one than this, than to lay
down one's life for his friends.

JOHN 15:12, 13 NKJV

A fool's wrath is known at once,
But a prudent man covers shame.

PROVERBS 12:16 NCV

Get along with each other, and forgive each other.
If someone does wrong to you, forgive that person because
the Lord forgave you.

COLOSSIANS 3:13 NCV

From what does such contrariness arise in habitually angry
people, but from a secret cause of too high an opinion of
themselves so that it pierces their hearts when they see any
man esteem them less than they esteem themselves?
An inflated estimation of ourselves is more than
half the weight of our wrath.

ST. THOMAS MORE

We are all fallen creatures and all very hard to live with.

C. S. LEWIS

A keen sense of humor helps us to overlook
the unbecoming, understand the unconventional,
tolerate the unpleasant, overcome the unexpected,
and outlast the unbearable.

BILLY GRAHAM

You are justified in avoiding people who send you from
their presence with less hope and strength to cope
with life's problems than when you met them.

ELLA WHEELER WILCOX

Additional Bible Readings

ROMANS 12:9-21; PHILIPPIANS 2:3, 4; ISAIAH 50:7-9A

DIVORCE

It's right there in black and white: Jesus clearly teaches that divorce is wrong: "If a man divorces his wife and marries another woman, he is guilty of adultery, and the man who marries a divorced woman is also guilty of adultery" (Luke 16: 18 NCV). And if that weren't clear enough, Jesus makes His point again with these familiar words: "What therefore God hath joined together, let not man put asunder" (Matthew 19:6 KJV). So there you have it: divorce is an affront to God's Word. Period. But we live in a world where divorce is an ever-present reality that touches countless families. So what are divorced people to do? The answer is straightforward: to ask God's forgiveness for any past failings, to "sin no more" (John 8:10, 11), and to seek, from this day forward, to live a life that is pleasing to Him.

If you are a divorced person, you may be experiencing a wide range of emotions: anger, pain, guilt, fear, and heartbreak, to name but a few. But even if you're struggling through the most difficult transition of your life, you must never lose faith. God remains faithful, and He's as near as your next heartbeat. As you turn to Him for guidance and support, here are a few things to consider:

1. God doesn't love divorce but He still loves you. It's certainly no secret: the Bible teaches that divorce is wrong. Yet we must remember that ours is a merciful and a loving

God. God loves you despite your shortcomings, and He loves you despite your divorce. (Romans 8:38, 39)

2. God isn't just near, He is here . . . and if you draw close to Him, He will draw close to you. (James 4:8)

3. God forgives sin when you ask . . . so ask! God stands ready to forgive . . . the next move is yours. (Psalm 51:1, 2; James 5:11; Acts 10:43)

4. Bitterness is poison. If you continue to harbor feelings of bitterness or regret, it's time to forgive everybody (including yourself). If you are unable to forgive, ask God to help you, and keep asking Him until He removes the poison of bitterness from your heart. (Matthew 6:14, 15; Matthew 7:7, 8)

5. The past is past, so don't live there. If you're focused on the past, change your focus. If you're living in the past, it's time to stop living there. (Isaiah 43:18, 19)

6. You can learn from your experience. If your last relationship was troublesome—or worse—learn from it, so that your next relationship won't be. (Proverbs 21:11)

7. God still has a wonderful plan for your life. And the time to start looking for that plan—and living it—is now. (Psalm 16:11)

The Lord God of Israel says, "I hate divorce."

MALACHI 2:16 NCV

If we confess our sins, He is faithful and just to forgive us our sins and to cleanse us from all unrighteousness.

1 JOHN 1:9 NKJV

For I am persuaded that neither death nor life, nor angels nor principalities nor powers, nor things present nor things to come, nor height nor depth, nor any other created thing, shall be able to separate us from the love of God which is in Christ Jesus our Lord.

ROMANS 8:38, 39 NKJV

Let us, then, feel very sure that we can come before God's throne where there is grace. There we can receive mercy and grace to help us when we need it.

HEBREWS 4:16 NCV

More Thoughts About . . . DIVORCE

God hates divorce, but He loves you.

JIM GALLERY

It doesn't matter how big the sin is or how small,
it doesn't matter whether it was spontaneous or malicious.
God will forgive you if you come to Him
and confess your sin!

ANNE GRAHAM LOTZ

When God forgives, He forgets. He buries our sins
in the sea and puts a sign on the shore saying,
"No Fishing Allowed."

CORRIE TEN BOOM

The fact is, God no longer deals with us in judgment but
in mercy. If people got what they deserved, this old planet
would have ripped apart at the seams centuries ago.
Praise God that because of His great love "we are not
consumed, for his compassions never fail (Lam. 3:22).

JONI EARECKSON TADA

Additional Bible Readings

1 CORINTHIANS 7:10-16; 2 CORINTHIANS 12:9; EPHESIANS 4:32;

EPHESIANS 5:21-33; MARK 10:2-8; PSALM 145:8, 9

FAMILY PROBLEMS

A loving family is a treasure from God. If you happen to be a member of a close knit, supportive clan, offer a word of thanks to your Creator. He has blessed you with one of His most precious earthy possessions. Your obligation, in response to God's gift, is to treat your family in ways that are consistent with His commandments.

No family is perfect, and neither, of course, is yours. When problems occur, as they will from time to time, here are a few things to remember:

1. Put God first in every aspect of your life. And while you're at it, put Him first in every aspect of your family's life, too. (Joshua 24:15)

2. Choose your words carefully. Harsh words are easy to speak and impossible to retrieve, so think before you speak. (Proverbs 12:18)

3. Know what to overlook. Until the day that you become perfect, don't expect them to be. (Luke 6:36)

4. Don't interfere with the logical consequences that accompany misbehavior. When you enable someone to continue misbehaving—whether that person is a child or an adult—you encourage continued misbehavior. So don't accept unacceptable behavior. (Hebrews 12:5, 6)

5. Don't be afraid to seek help. If you're facing family problems that you just can't seem to solve, don't hesitate to consult your pastor or an experienced counselor. (Proverbs 1:5)

6. Don't give up on God. And remember: He will never give up on you or your family. (Hebrews 10:23)

In spite of the inevitable challenges of family life, your clan is God's gift to you. That little band of men, women, kids, and babies comprises a treasure on temporary loan from the Father above. As you prayerfully seek God's direction, remember that He has important plans for you and yours. It's up to you to live—and to love—accordingly.

*Choose for yourselves this day whom you will serve,
whether the gods which your fathers served that were on
the other side of the River, or the gods of the Amorites,
in whose land you dwell. But as for me and my house,
we will serve the Lord."*

JOSHUA 24:15 NKJV

*Children, obey your parents in the Lord, for this is
right. "Honor your father and mother," which is the first
commandment with promise: "that it may be well with you
and you may live long on the earth." And you, fathers,
do not provoke your children to wrath, but bring them up in
the training and admonition of the Lord.*

EPHESIANS 6:1-4 NKJV

*Let all bitterness, wrath, anger, clamor, and evil speaking
be put away from you, with all malice. And be kind to one
another, tenderhearted, forgiving one another,
just as God in Christ forgave you.*

EPHESIANS 4:31, 32 NKJV

Money can build or buy a house. Add love to that, and you have a home. Add God to that, and you have a temple. You have "a little colony of the kingdom of heaven."

ANNE ORTLAND

What can we do to promote world peace?
Go home and love your family.

MOTHER TERESA

Creating a warm, caring, supportive, encouraging environment is probably the most important thing you can do for your family.

STEPHEN COVEY

It is a reverent thing to see an ancient castle or building not in decay, or to see a fair timber tree sound and perfect. How much more beautiful it is to behold an ancient and noble family that has stood against the waves and weathers of time.

FRANCIS BACON

Additional Bible Readings

DEUTERONOMY 6:6-9; EPHESIANS 5:22-29; EXODUS 20:12;

PROVERBS 22:6; PROVERBS 29:17; PSALM 127:5

FORGIVENESS

Life would be much simpler if we could forgive people "once and for all" and be done with it. But forgiveness is seldom that easy. For most of us, the decision to forgive is straightforward, but the process of forgiving is more difficult. Forgiveness is a journey that requires effort, time, perseverance, and prayer.

Forgiveness is seldom easy, but it is always right. When we forgive those who have hurt us, we honor God by obeying His commandments. But when we harbor bitterness against others, we disobey God—with predictably unhappy results.

Sometimes, it's not "the other guy" that you need to forgive; it's yourself. If you've made mistakes—and who among us hasn't?—perhaps you're continuing to bear a grudge against the person in the mirror. If so, here's a three-step process for resolving those feelings: 1. Stop the harmful behavior that is the source of your self-directed anger. 2. Seek forgiveness from God (and from any people you may have hurt). 3. Ask God to cleanse your heart of all bitterness and regret . . . and keep asking Him until He does.

If there exists even one person, alive or dead, whom you have not forgiven (and that includes yourself), follow God's commandment and His will for your life: forgive that person today. And remember that bitterness, anger, and regret are not part of God's plan for your life. Forgiveness is.

Are you easily frustrated by the inevitable shortcomings

of others? Are you a prisoner of bitterness or regret? If so, perhaps you need a refresher course in the art of forgiveness. If you are imprisoned by the chains of anger and bitterness, it's time to embark upon a journey of forgiveness. You begin that journey by redirecting your thoughts and your prayers. If you sincerely wish to forgive someone, pray for that person. And then pray for yourself by asking God to heal your heart. Don't expect forgiveness to be easy or quick, but rest assured: with God as your partner, you can forgive . . . and you will.

God's Word About . . . **FORGIVENESS**

---

*If you forgive others for their sins, your Father in heaven will
also forgive you for your sins. But if you don't forgive others,
your Father in heaven will not forgive your sins.*

MATTHEW 6:14, 15 NCV

*Then Peter came to Him and said, "Lord, how often shall
my brother sin against me, and I forgive him?
Up to seven times?" Jesus said to him,
"I do not say to you, up to seven times,
but up to seventy times seven."*

MATTHEW 18:21, 22 NKJV

*"The Spirit of the Lord God is upon Me, Because the Lord has
anointed Me To preach good tidings to the poor;
He has sent Me to heal the brokenhearted,
To proclaim liberty to the captives,
And the opening of the prison to those who are bound.*

ISAIAH 61:1 NKJV

*For I will be merciful to their unrighteousness,
and their sins and their lawless deeds
I will remember no more."*

HEBREWS 8:12 NKJV

More Thoughts About . . . **FORGIVENESS**

God calls upon the loved not just to love but
to be loving. God calls upon the forgiven
not just to forgive but to be forgiving.

BETH MOORE

Give me such love for God and men as will blot out
all hatred and bitterness.

DIETRICH BONHOEFFER

Looking back over my life, all I can see is mercy and
grace written in large letters everywhere.
May God help me have the same kind of heart toward
those who wound or offend me.

JIM CYMBALA

I believe that forgiveness can become a continuing cycle:
because God forgives us, we're to forgive others;
because we forgive others, God forgives us.
Scripture presents both parts of the cycle.

SHIRLEY DOBSON

Additional Bible Readings

I JOHN 1:9; COLOSSIANS 3:13; EPHESIANS 4:31, 32; ISAIAH 43:25;

JEREMIAH 3:8; LUKE 6: 36, 37; ROMANS 12:19, 20; PSALM 103:12

GUILT

All of us have sinned. Sometimes our sins result from our own stubborn rebellion against God's commandments. Sometimes, we are swept up by events that encourage us to behave in ways that we later come to regret. And sometimes, even when our intentions are honorable, we make mistakes that have long-lasting consequences. When we look back at our actions with remorse, we may experience intense feelings of guilt. But God has an answer for the guilt that we feel. That answer, of course, is His forgiveness.

When we genuinely repent from our wrongdoings, and when we sincerely confess our sins, we are forgiven by our Heavenly Father. But sometimes, long after God has forgiven us, we may continue to withhold forgiveness from ourselves. Instead of accepting God's mercy and accepting our past, we may think long and hard—far too long and hard—about the things that "might have been," the things that "could have been," or the things that "should have been."

Are you troubled by feelings of guilt, even after you've received God's forgiveness? Are you still struggling with painful memories of mistakes you made long ago? Are you focused so intently on yesterday that your vision of today is clouded? If so, you still have work to do—spiritual work. You should ask your Heavenly Father not for forgiveness (He granted that gift the very first time you asked Him!) but instead for acceptance and trust: acceptance of the past and trust in God's plan for your life.

If you find yourself plagued by feelings of guilt or shame, consult God's survival guide: His Holy Word. And as you do so, consider the following Biblically-based tips for overcoming those feelings of guilt once and for all:

1. Stop doing the things that make you feel guilty: How can you expect not to feel guilty if you should feel guilty? (Acts 26:20)

2. Ask God for forgiveness. When you ask for it, He will give it. (1 John 1:9)

3. Ask forgiveness from the people you have harmed: This step is hard, but helpful. And even if the other folks cannot find it in their hearts to forgive you, you have the satisfaction of knowing you that you asked. (Proverbs 28:13)

4. Forgive yourself: if you're no longer misbehaving, it's the right thing to do. And today is the right day to do it. (Romans 14:22)

5. Become more diligent in your daily time of prayer and Bible study. A regular time of quiet reflection and prayer will allow you to praise your Creator, to focus your thoughts, to remind yourself of His love, and to seek His guidance in matters great and small. (Isaiah 50:4, 5)

6. Get busy making the world a better place. Now that God has forgiven you, it's time for you to show your gratitude by serving Him. (Matthew 23:11, 12)

---

*There is therefore now no condemnation to those who are
in Christ Jesus, who do not walk according to the flesh,
but according to the Spirit.*

ROMANS 8:1 NKJV

*Then I confessed my sins to you and didn't hide my guilt.
I said, "I will confess my sins to the Lord,"
and you forgave my guilt.*

PSALM 32:5 NCV

*For if you return to the Lord, your brethren and your children
will be treated with compassion by those who lead them captive,
so that they may come back to this land; for the Lord your God
is gracious and merciful, and will not turn His face
from you if you return to Him."*

2 CHRONICLES 30:9 NKJV

*I have blotted out, like a thick cloud, your transgressions,
And like a cloud, your sins. Return to Me,
for I have redeemed you."*

ISAIAH 44:22 NKJV

More Thoughts About . . . **GUILT**

You never lose the love of God. Guilt is the warning
that temporarily you are out of touch.

JACK DOMINIAN

Spiritual life without guilt would be like physical life
without pain. Guilt is a defense mechanism;
it's like an alarm that goes off to lead you
to confession when you sin.

JOHN MACARTHUR

Let's take Jesus at this word. When he says we're forgiven,
let's unload the guilt. When he says we're valuable,
let's believe him. When he says we're eternal,
let's bury our fear. When he says we're provided for,
let's stop worrying.

MAX LUCADO

Satan knows that if you live under a dark cloud of guilt,
you will not be able to witness effectively or
serve the Lord with power and blessing.

WARREN WIERSBE

Guilt is the gift that keeps on giving.

ERMA BOMBECK

Additional Bible Readings

2 CORINTHIANS 7:10; MICAH 7:18,19; PSALM 32:5; PSALM 103:9-12;

ROMANS 8:35; 38, 39; ROMANS 3:23

LONELINESS

If you're like most people, you've experienced occasional bouts of loneliness. If so, you understand the genuine pain that accompanies those feelings that "nobody cares." In truth, lots of people care about you, but at times, you may hardly notice their presence.

Sometimes, intense feelings of loneliness are the result of depression (please read the discussion on this topic in Part I of this book). Other times, however, your feelings of loneliness come as a result of your own hesitation: the hesitation to "get out there and make new friends."

Why do so many of us hesitate to meet new people and make new friends? Several reasons: some of us are just plain shy, and because of our shyness, we find it more difficult to interact with unfamiliar people. Others, while not exceedingly shy, are overly attuned to the potential of rejection (a fear that is discussed later in Part II of this text). Still others may be so self-critical that they feel unworthy of the attentions of others.

In truth, the world is literally teeming with people who are looking for new friends. And yet, ironically enough, too many of us allow our friendships to wither away, not because we intentionally alienate others, but because we simply don't pay enough attention to them.

The philosopher William James observed, "Human beings are born into this little span of life, and among the best things that life has to offer are its friendships and intimacies. Yet, humans leave their friendships with no cultivation, letting them grow as they will by the roadside." James understood that when we leave our friendships unattended, the resulting harvest is predictably slim.

Ralph Waldo Emerson advised, "The only way to have a friend is to be one." Emerson realized that a lasting relationship, like a beautiful garden, must be tended with care. Here are a few helpful tips on tending the garden of friendship . . . and reaping a bountiful harvest:

1. Remember the first rule of friendship: it's the Golden one, and it starts like this: "Do unto others . . ." (Matthew 7:12)

2. If you're trying to make new friends, become interested in them . . . and eventually they'll become interested in you. (Colossians 3:12)

3. Take the time to reconnect with old friends: they'll be glad you did, and so, too, will you. (Philippians 1:3)

4. Become more involved in your church or in community service: they'll welcome your participation, and you'll welcome the chance to connect with more and more people. (1 Peter 5:2)

Have I not commanded you? Be strong and of good courage;
do not be afraid, nor be dismayed,
for the Lord your God is with you wherever you go.

JOSHUA 1:9 NKJV

Draw near to God and He will draw near to you.

JAMES 4:8 NKJV

Do not be unequally yoked together with unbelievers.
For what fellowship has righteousness with lawlessness?
And what communion has light with darkness?

2 CORINTHIANS 6:14 NKJV

Beloved, if God so loved us,
we also ought to love one another.

1 JOHN 4:11 NKJV

More Thoughts About . . . LONELINESS

As we focus on His love and Word, in time He will fill
our void and loneliness, and He will heal our pain.

ANITA CORRINE DONIHUE

Loneliness is the first thing which God's eye
named not good.

JOHN MILTON

Be patient. When you feel lonely, stay with your loneliness.
Avoid the temptation to let your fearful self run off.
Let it teach you its wisdom; let it tell you that you can live
instead of just surviving. Gradually you will become one,
and you will find that Jesus is living in your heart
and offering you all you need.

HENRI NOUWEN

It is an act of the will to allow God to be our refuge.
Otherwise, we live outside of his love and protection,
wondering why we feel alone and afraid.

MARY MORRISON SUGGS

Additional Bible Readings

PROVERBS 27:10; PROVERBS 27:17; PSALM 139:7-10

RELATIONSHIP PROBLEMS

AND MARRIAGE DIFFICULTIES

Emotional health is contagious, and so is emotional distress. If you're fortunate enough to be surrounded by family members and friends who celebrate life and praise God, consider yourself profoundly blessed. But, if you find yourself caught in an unhealthy relationship, it's time to look realistically at your situation and begin making changes.

Don't worry about changing your spouse: no matter how hard you try, you probably can't do it. Your spouse will change when he or she is ready to change, and not before. What you can do is this: You can conduct yourself in a responsible fashion and insist that other people treat you with the dignity and consideration that you deserve.

In a perfect world filled with perfect people, our relationships, too, would be perfect. But none of us is perfect and neither are our relationships . . . and that's okay. As we work to make our imperfect relationships a little happier and healthier, we grow as individuals and as families. And here are a few tips that, if taken to heart, can improve any relationship, including yours:

1. Take the words of 1 Corinthians 13:13 to heart: "And now abide faith, hope, love, these three; but the greatest of these is love." (NKJV)

2. Be patient...very patient: Want them to be patient with you? Then you must do the same for them (Proverbs 19:11)

3. Get Plenty of Rest: If you're burning the candle at both ends, you'll be grumpy, you'll be exhausted, and you won't think very clearly. So do you loved ones a favor: snuff out one end of the candle and go to bed. (Matthew 11:28)

4. Communicate wisely and often: Avoid shouting matches and encourage honest dialogue. (Proverbs 25:11)

5. Be Cooperative: remember that the two of you are "in this thing" together, so play like teammates, not rivals. (Matthew 12:25)

6. Be Encouraging: The words from the old cowboy song are familiar: "And seldom is heard a discouraging word...." And if it's good enough for Home on the Range, it's good enough for your home, too. Make certain that your little abode is a haven of encouragement for every member of your clan. You do so by checking your gripes and disappointments at the front door...and encouraging everybody else to do likewise! (Hebrews 3:13)

7. Honesty Matters: Trust is the foundation of meaningful relationships. If you want your relationship to last, be honest and trustworthy. If you want a second or third-class relationship, be deceptive, evasive, and sneaky. (Proverbs 28:18)

8. Forgive and Keep Forgiving: If you're having trouble forgiving your loved ones, think of all the times your loved ones have forgiven you! (1 Peter 4:8)

9. Put God Where He Belongs—First: Any relationship that doesn't honor God is a relationship that is destined for problems, and soon. (Hebrews 12:2)

LET NOT MERCY AND TRUTH
FORSAKE YOU;
BIND THEM AROUND YOUR NECK,
WRITE THEM ON THE TABLET
OF YOUR HEART.

—

PROVERBS 3:3

THERE IS NOTHING WRONG WITH A MARRIAGE THAT SACRIFICE WOULDN'T HEAL.

—

ELISABETH ELLIOT

*Let the husband render to his wife the affection due her,
and likewise also the wife to her husband.*

1 CORINTHIANS 7:3 NKJV

*Wives, yield to the authority of your husbands,
because this is the right thing to do in the Lord.
Husbands, love your wives and be gentle with them.*

COLOSSIANS 3:18, 19 NCV

*But each one of you must love his wife as he loves himself,
and a wife must respect her husband.*

EPHESIANS 5:33 NCV

*Therefore a man shall leave his father and mother
and be joined to his wife, and they shall become one flesh.*

GENESIS 2:24 NKJV

Those who abandon ship the first time it enters
a storm miss the calm beyond. And the rougher
the storms weathered together,
the deeper and stronger real love grows.

RUTH BELL GRAHAM

Husbands and wives who live happily ever after learn to
give and take and to reach agreement by mutual consent.
A man or woman with an unmovable backbone is in real
trouble. God made backbones that can stand rigid
but can also bend when necessary.

VANCE HAVNER

Eve was not taken from the feet of Adam to be his slave,
nor from his head to be his lord,
but from his side to be his partner.

PETER LOMBARD

We've grown to be one soul—two parts; our lives are
so intertwined that when some passion stirs your heart,
I feel the quake in mine.

GLORIA GAITHER

Additional Bible Readings

HEBREWS 13:4; PROVERBS 12:4; PROVERBS 18:22;

PROVERBS 31:10; PROVERBS 31:30, 31

REJECTION

The fear of rejection and its first cousin, the fear of failure, are roadblocks on the path to a purposeful life. When we try to please everybody in sight, we create for ourselves a task that is unrealistic, unsatisfying, and unworthy of our efforts. A far better strategy, of course, is to concentrate, first and foremost, on pleasing God. But sometimes, that's easier said than done, especially for folks who focus too intently on being "people pleasers."

Pleasing other people is a good thing . . . up to a point. Being a kind and considerate person is, of course, an important part of being a good Christian. But, we should never allow our "willingness to please" to interfere with our own good judgement or with God's commandments.

If you're a world-class people-pleaser, and if you're displeased with the consequences of your behavior, consider the following:

1. Your fear of rejection probably results from unspoken (yet highly pervasive) messages that you're telling yourself about the consequences of being judged "unworthy" or "imperfect" by the people whom you seek to impress. If so, it's time to start thinking more about impressing God and less about impressing your pals. (2 Corinthians 5:9, 10)

2. You may be living and laboring under the mistaken belief that it is "horrible" or "awful" to hear the word "no." Far too many people put their lives on hold because they fear being turned down by others. If the fear of the little two-letter word "no" is standing between you and the things you want from life, proceed ahead in spite of your fears. When you do, you'll soon discover that the rewards of facing rejection far outweigh the risks. (Psalm 56:3)

3. Look for ways that your fear of rejection may impact other areas of your life: Are you a procrastinator? Perhaps you're afraid that your work (and, by implication, yourself) will be judged as "imperfect." Are you stuck in an unrewarding (or unhealthy) dating relationship? Perhaps you're overly afraid of displeasing the other person by breaking things off (even if the other person is mistreating you). Is your career stuck in neutral? Perhaps the fear of rejection has interfered with your need to search for a better job. Did you go dateless to the prom? Perhaps you were so afraid of being turned down that you never got around to asking anybody to go with you! From these few examples, it's clear that the fear of rejection can affect many areas of your life. That's why it's important that you think rationally and honestly about your relationships, your behaviors, your habits, and your life. (Romans 12:2)

4. You can't please everybody, nor should you even try. Of course there are a few people whom you should seek to please, starting with your family (and, to a lesser extent, the person who signs your paycheck). But, trying to please everybody else is an impossible, all-consuming task that will complicate your life, deplete your energies, and leave you unhappy, unappreciated, and unfulfilled. So focus your thoughts and energies on pleasing your Father in Heaven first and always. And when it comes to the world and all its inhabitants, don't worry too much about the folks you can't please; focus instead on doing the right thing—and leave the rest up to God. (Galatians 1:10)

And whoever will not receive you nor hear you,
when you depart from there, shake off the dust under your feet
as a testimony against them.

MARK 6:11 NKJV

Now all things are of God, who has reconciled us to
Himself through Jesus Christ, and
has given us the ministry of reconciliation.

2 CORINTHIANS 5:18 NKJV

Do you think I am trying to make people accept me?
No, God is the One I am trying to please.
Am I trying to please people? If I still wanted to please people,
I would not be a servant of Christ.

GALATIANS 1:10 NCV

As for myself, I do not care if I am judged by you or by any
human court. I do not even judge myself. I know of no wrong
I have done, but this does not make me right before the Lord.
The Lord is the One who judges me.

1 CORINTHIANS 4:3, 4 NCV

When we are set free from the bondage of pleasing others, when we are free from currying others' favor and others' approval—then no one will be able to make us miserable or dissatisfied. And then, if we know we have pleased God, contentment will be our consolation.

KAY ARTHUR

You should forget about trying to be popular with everybody and start trying to be popular with God Almighty.

SAM JONES

When you taste a measure of being able to love and enjoy the people in your life, without having to have any particular response from them, you are tasting bliss.

PAULA RINEHART

Pride opens the door to every other sin, for once we are more concerned with our reputation than our character, there is no end to the things we will do just to make ourselves "look good" before others.

WARREN WIERSBE

Additional Bible Readings

2 TIMOTHY 2:4; PROVERBS 11:25; TITUS 3:9

PART III

LEARNING HOW TO LIVE

Life has important lessons to teach us. It's up to each of us to learn those lessons as best we can and then to share them.

In Part III of God's Survival Guide, we consider an assortment of 21st-Century problems along with time-tested, Biblically-based solutions. If you seek to improve your own life and the lives of your loved ones, the ideas on the following pages can help.

ADDICTION

The dictionary defines addiction as "the compulsive need for a habit-forming substance; the condition of being habitually and compulsively occupied with something." That definition is accurate, but incomplete. For Christians, addiction has an additional meaning: it means compulsively worshipping something other than God.

Ours is a highly addictive society. Why? The answer is straightforward: supply and demand. The supply of addictive substances continues to grow; the affordability and availability of these substances makes them highly attractive to consumers; and the overall demand for addictive substances has increased as more and more users have become addicted to an ever-expanding array of substances and compulsions.

The list of addictive products is extensive: alcohol, drugs (illegal and prescription varieties), cigarettes, gambling (often government-sponsored), sex (an age-old profession with a new twist: on-line pornography), and food (100 years ago, overeating would not have qualified as a major addiction, but oh, how things have changed).

Unless you're living on a deserted island, you know people who are full-blown addicts—probably lots of people. If you, or someone you love, is suffering from the blight of addiction, the following ideas are worth remembering:

1. For the addict, addiction comes first. In the life of an addict, addiction rules. God, of course, commands otherwise.

God says, "You shall have no other gods before Me," and He means precisely what He says (Exodus 20:3 NKJV). Our task, as believers, is to put God in His proper place: first place.

2. You cannot cure another person's addiction, but you can encourage that person to seek help. Addicts are cured when they decide, not when you decide. What you can do is this: You can be supportive, and you can encourage the addict to find the help that he or she needs. (Luke 10:25-37)

3. If you are living with an addicted person, think about safety: yours and your family's. Addiction is life-threatening and life-shortening. Don't let someone else's addiction threaten your safety or the safety of your loved ones. (Proverbs 22:3)

4. Don't assist in prolonging the addiction: When you interfere with the negative consequences that might otherwise accompany an addict's negative behaviors, you are inadvertently "enabling" the addict to continue the destructive cycle of addiction. So don't be an enabler. (Proverbs 15:31)

5. Help is available: Lots of people have experienced addiction and lived to tell about it. They want to help. Let them. (Proverbs 27:17)

6. Cure is possible. With God's help, no addiction is incurable. And with God, no situation is hopeless. (Matthew 19:26)

Don't drink too much wine or eat too much food.
Those who drink and eat too much become poor.
They sleep too much and end up wearing rags.

PROVERBS 23: 20, 21 NCV

For we do not have a High Priest who cannot sympathize
with our weaknesses, but was in all points tempted as we are,
yet without sin. Let us therefore come boldly to
the throne of grace, that we may obtain mercy
and find grace to help in time of need.

HEBREWS 4:15, 16 NKJV

Yet in all these things we are more than conquerors
through Him who loved us.

ROMANS 8:37 NKJV

Therefore submit to God. Resist the devil and he will flee
from you. Draw near to God and He will draw near to you.
Cleanse your hands, you sinners; and purify your hearts,
you double-minded.

JAMES 4: 7, 8 NKJV

Addiction is the most powerful psychic enemy of
humanity's desire for God.

GERALD MAY

The soul that journeys to God, but doesn't shake off
its cares and quiet its appetites, is like someone
who drags a cart uphill.

ST. JOHN OF THE CROSS

You will become as small as your controlling desire;
as great as your dominant aspiration.

JAMES ALLEN

The more you give your mental burdens to the Lord,
the more exciting it becomes to see how God will handle
things that are impossible for you to do anything about.

CHARLES SWINDOLL

Additional Bible Readings

JOB 36:15; LUKE 21:34-36; MATTHEW 7:7, 8; PHILIPPIANS 4:13;

PROVERBS 23:29-35

BUSYNESS

Has the busy pace of life robbed you of the peace that might otherwise be yours through Jesus Christ? If so, you are simply too busy for your own good. Through His only begotten Son, God offers you a peace that passes human understanding, but He won't force His peace upon you; in order to experience it, you must slow down long enough to sense His presence and His love.

Time is a nonrenewable gift from God. How will you use it? You know from experience that you should invest some time each day in yourself, but finding time to do so is easier said than done. As a busy Christian, you may have difficulty investing large blocks of time in much-needed thought and self-reflection. If so, it may be time to reorder your priorities.

"First things first" is an adage that's easy to speak but hard to put into practice. Why? Because we live in a demanding world, a world filled with distractions and temptations. And as we try to prioritize our days and our lives, we are confronted by so many people who are expecting so many things from us! But we must never allow ourselves to become so busy that we fail to make time for God.

God has big plans for you. Discovering those plans will require trial and error, meditation and prayer, faith and perseverance. The moments of silence that you claim for yourself will help you gather your thoughts and sense direction from your Creator.

Each waking moment holds the potential to think a creative thought or offer a heartfelt prayer. So even if you're a person with too many demands and too few hours in which to meet them, don't panic. Instead, be comforted in the knowledge that when you sincerely seek to discover God's priorities for your life, He will provide answers in marvelous and surprising ways.

Remember: this is the day that God has made and that He has filled it with countless opportunities to love, to serve, and to seek His guidance. Seize those opportunities today, and keep seizing them every day that you live. And as a gift to yourself, to your family, and to the world, slow down and claim the inner peace that is your spiritual birthright: the peace of Jesus Christ. It is offered freely; it has been paid for in full; it is yours for the asking. So ask. And then share.

Be still, and know that I am God;
I will be exalted among the nations,
I will be exalted in the earth!

PSALM 46:10 NKJV

He makes me to lie down in green pastures;
He leads me beside the still waters. He restores my soul;
He leads me in the paths of righteousness For His name's sake.

PSALM 23:2, 3 NKJV

From the end of the earth I will cry to You,
When my heart is overwhelmed;
Lead me to the rock that is higher than I.

PSALM 61:2 NKJV

But seek first the kingdom of God and His righteousness,
and all these things shall be added to you.

MATTHEW 6:33 NKJV

More Thoughts About . . . **BUSYNESS**

The foe of opportunity is preoccupation. Just when God
sends along a chance to turn a great victory for mankind,
some of us are too busy puttering around to notice it.

A. W. TOZER

You're busy with all the pressures of the world around you,
but in that busyness you're missing the most important
element of all—God's ongoing presence
that is available to you.

BILL HYBELS

Noise and words and frenzied, hectic schedules dull
our senses, closing our ears to His still, small voice and
making us numb to His touch.

CHARLES SWINDOLL

God is more concerned with the direction of your life
than with its speed.

MARIE T. FREEMAN

Busyness is the great enemy of relationships.

RICK WARREN

Additional Bible Readings

ISAIAH 30:15; PSALM 19:14; PSALM 37:7; PSALM 62:5

DEALING WITH CHANGE

Our world is in a state of constant change. God is not. At times, the world seems to be trembling beneath our feet. But we can be comforted in the knowledge that our Heavenly Father is the rock that cannot be shaken. His Word promises, "I am the Lord, I do not change" (Malachi 3:6 NKJV).

Every day that we live, we mortals encounter a multitude of changes—some good, some not so good, and some downright disheartening. On those occasions when we must endure life-changing personal losses that leave us breathless, there is a place we can turn for comfort and assurance—we can turn to God. When we do, our loving Heavenly Father stands ready to protect us, to comfort us, to guide us, and, in time, to heal us.

Are you facing difficult circumstances or unwelcome changes? If so, please remember that God is far bigger than any problem you may face. So, instead of worrying about life's inevitable challenges, put your faith in the Father and His only begotten Son: "Jesus Christ is the same yesterday, today, and forever" (Hebrews 13:8 NKJV). And remember: it is precisely because your Savior does not change that you can face your challenges with courage for today and hope for tomorrow.

Life is often challenging, but as Christians, we should not be afraid. God loves us, and He will protect us. In times of hardship, He will comfort us; in times of change, He will guide our steps. When we are troubled, or weak, or sorrowful, God is always with us. We must build our lives on the rock that cannot be moved…we must trust in God. Always.

Are you anxious about situations that you cannot control? Take your anxieties to God. Are you troubled about changes that threaten to disrupt your life? Take your troubles to Him. Does your corner of the world seem to be trembling beneath your feet? Seek protection from the One who cannot be moved. The same God who created the universe will protect you if you ask Him . . . so ask Him . . . and then serve Him with willing hands and a trusting heart.

So don't worry about tomorrow, because tomorrow will have
its own worries. Each day has enough trouble of its own.

MATTHEW 6:34 NCV

Though an army may encamp against me,
My heart shall not fear; Though war should rise against me,
In this I will be confident. One thing I have desired of the Lord,
That will I seek: That I may dwell in the house of the Lord
All the days of my life, To behold the beauty of the Lord,
And to inquire in His temple. For in the time of trouble He shall
hide me in His pavilion; In the secret place of His tabernacle
He shall hide me; He shall set me high upon a rock.

PSALM 27:3-5 NKJV

I leave you peace; my peace I give you. I do not give it to you
as the world does. So don't let your hearts be troubled or afraid.

JOHN 14:27 NCV

The Lord is my rock and my fortress and my deliverer;
My God, my strength, in whom I will trust;
My shield and the horn of my salvation, my stronghold.

PSALM 18:2 NKJV

But I'm convinced the best way to cope with change,
ironically enough, is to get to know a God
who doesn't change, One who provides an anchor
in the swirling seas of change.

BILL HYBELS

Conditions are always changing; therefore, I must not be
dependent upon conditions. What matters supremely is
my soul and my relationship to God.

CORRIE TEN BOOM

Christians are supposed not merely to endure change,
nor even to profit by it, but to cause it.

HARRY EMERSON FOSDICK

GOD, grant me the serenity to accept the things I cannot
change, the courage to change the things I can,
and the wisdom to know the difference.

REINHOLD NIEBUHR

Additional Bible Readings

ISAIAH 12:2; ECCLESIASTES 3:1; PHILIPPIANS 4:11, 12;

PROVERBS 27:12; PSALM 46:1

DEATH OF A LOVED ONE

In time, grief visits us all. When we experience the loss of a loved one, we may experience pain is that is so deep and so profound that we honestly wonder if recovery is possible. But with God, all things are possible, and no situation is hopeless. The Christian faith, as communicated through the words of the Holy Bible, is a healing faith. It offers comfort in times of trouble, courage instead of fear, hope instead of hopelessness.

For Christians, death is not an ending; it is a beginning. For Christian believers, the grave is not a final resting-place; it is a place of transition. Yet even when we know our loved ones are at peace with Christ, we still weep bitter tears, not so much for the departed as for ourselves.

Through the healing words of God's promises, Christians understand that the Lord continues to manifest His plan in good times and bad. God promises that He is "close to the brokenhearted" (Psalm 34:18). In times of intense sadness, we must turn to Him, and we must encourage our friends and family members to do likewise.

If you are experiencing the intense pain of a recent loss, or if you are still mourning a loss from long ago, it's time to revisit God's promises. And as you do so, the following ideas can help:

1. Grief is not meant to be avoided or feared; it is meant to be worked through. Grief hurts, but denying your true feelings can hurt even more. With God's help, you can face your pain and move beyond it. (Psalm 118:5, 6)

2. The grieving process takes time: God does not promise instantaneous healing, but He does promise healing: "I have heard your prayer, I have seen your tears; surely I will heal you." (2 Kings 20:5 NKJV)

3. Other people have experienced grief that is similar to yours, and they are willing to help: let them. (Matthew 5:4)

4. In time, God will dry your tears if you let Him: And if you haven't already allowed Him to begin His healing process, today is a perfect day to start. (Psalm 147:3)

5. You can use your own suffering as a way to help others—and at the appropriate time, that's precisely what you should do. (Galatians 6:2)

And God will wipe away every tear from their eyes;
there shall be no more death, nor sorrow, nor crying.
There shall be no more pain, for the former things
have passed away.

REVELATION 21:4 NKJV

"Let not your heart be troubled; you believe in God,
believe also in Me. In My Father's house are many mansions;
if it were not so, I would have told you. I go to prepare
a place for you. And if I go and prepare a place for you,
I will come again and receive you to Myself; that where I am,
there you may be also.

JOHN 14:1-3 NKJV

We are confident, yes, well pleased rather to be absent from
the body and to be present with the Lord.

2 CORINTHIANS 5:8 NKJV

But I do not want you to be ignorant, brethren, concerning
those who have fallen asleep, lest you sorrow as others who have
no hope. For if we believe that Jesus died and rose again,
even so God will bring with Him those who sleep in Jesus.

1 THESSALONIANS 4:13, 14 NKJV

Mercy is not the ability to no longer feel the pain and heartache of living in this world. Mercy is knowing that I am being held through the pain by my Father.

ANGELA THOMAS

One of the more significant things God will bring out of our grief and depression is an ability to walk constructively with others through theirs. In fact, one of the purposes of God's comfort is to equip us to comfort others.

DAVID B. BIEBEL

Even in the winter, even in the midst of the storm, the sun is still there. Somewhere, up above the clouds, it still shines and warms and pulls at the life buried deep inside the brown branches and frozen earth.
The sun is there! Spring will come.

GLORIA GAITHER

Additional Bible Readings

1 CORINTHIANS 15:55-57; HEBREWS 10:23; JOHN 5:24, 25;

PSALM 116:1-4; PSALM 23

DIFFICULT DECISIONS

Life is a series of choices. From the instant we wake in the morning until the moment we nod off to sleep at night, we make countless decisions: decisions about the things we do, decisions about the words we speak, and decisions about the thoughts we choose to think. Simply put, the quality of those decisions determines the quality of our lives.

Some decisions are easy to make because the consequences of those decisions are small. When the person behind the counter asks, "Want fries with that?" the necessary response requires little thought because the consequences of that decision are minor.

Some decisions, on the other hand, are big . . . very big. The biggest decision, of course, is one that far too many people ignore: the decision concerning God's only begotten Son. But if you're a believer in Christ, you've already made that choice, and you have received God's gift of grace. Perhaps now you're asking yourself "What's next, Lord?" If so, you may be facing a series of big decisions concerning your life and your future. Here are some things you can do:

1. Gather as much information as you can: don't expect to get all the facts—that's impossible—but get as many facts as you can in a reasonable amount of time. (Proverbs 24:3, 4)

2. Don't be too impulsive: If you have time to make a decision, use that time to make a good decision. (Proverbs 19:2)

3. Rely on the advice of trusted friends and mentors. Proverbs 1:5 makes it clear: "A wise man will hear and increase learning, and a man of understanding will attain wise counsel." (NKJV)

4. Pray for guidance. When you seek it, He will give it. (Luke 11:9)

5. Trust the quiet inner voice of your conscience: Treat your conscience as you would a trusted advisor. (Luke 17:21)

6. When the time for action arrives, act. Procrastination is the enemy of progress; don't let it defeat you. (James 1:22)

I will instruct you and teach you in the way you should go;
I will guide you with My eye.

PSALM 32:8 NKJV

Trust in the Lord with all your heart, And lean not on your own
understanding; In all your ways acknowledge Him,
And He shall direct your paths.

PROVERBS 3:5, 6 NKJV

Now this is the confidence that we have in Him, that if we ask
anything according to His will, He hears us. And if we know
that He hears us, whatever we ask, we know that we have
the petitions that we have asked of Him.

1 JOHN 5:14, 15 NKJV

The way of a fool is right in his own eyes,
But he who heeds counsel is wise.

PROVERBS 12:15 NKJV

There is no need to fear the decisions of life when you
know Jesus Christ, for His name is Counselor.

WARREN WIERSBE

He who is his own guide is guided by a fool.

C. H. SPURGEON

There may be no trumpet sound or loud applause when
we make a right decision, just a calm sense of
resolution and peace.

GLORIA GAITHER

The Reference Point for the Christian is the Bible.
All values, judgments, and attitudes must be gauged in
relationship to this Reference Point.

RUTH BELL GRAHAM

Additional Bible Readings

JOSHUA 1:8; JOSHUA 24:15; PROVERBS 16:3; PSALM 94:19

FEAR OF THE FUTURE AND RISKING FAILURE

To his adoring fans, he was the "Sultan of Swat." He was Babe Ruth, the one-of-a-kind baseball legend who set records for both home runs and strikeouts. Babe's philosophy was simple. He said, "Never let the fear of striking out get in your way." That's smart advice on the diamond or off.

Of course it's never wise to take foolish risks (so buckle up, slow down, and don't do anything stupid!) But when it comes to the game of life, you should not let the fear of failure keep you from taking your swings.

THE TEMPTATION TO PLAY IT SAFE

As we consider the uncertainties of the future, we are confronted with a powerful temptation: the temptation to "play it safe." Unwilling to move mountains, we fret over molehills. Unwilling to entertain great hopes for tomorrow, we focus on the unfairness of today. Unwilling to trust God completely, we take timid half-steps when God intends that we make giant leaps. Why are we willing to settle for baby steps when God wants us to leap tall buildings in a single bound? Because we are fearful that we might fail.

The occasional disappointments and failures of life are inevitable. Such setbacks are simply the price that we must occasionally pay for our willingness to take risks as we follow our dreams. But even when we encounter bitter disappointments, we must never lose faith. And we must remember that in the game of life, we never hit a home run unless we are willing to step up to the plate and swing.

LIVING AND LEARNING

We are imperfect beings living in an imperfect world; mistakes are simply part of the price we pay for being here. Yet, even though mistakes are an inevitable part of life's journey, repeated mistakes should not be. When we commit the inevitable blunders of life, we must correct them, learn from them, and pray for the wisdom to avoid those same mistakes in the future. When we do so, our missteps become lessons, our lives become adventures in growth, and our stumbling blocks become stepping-stones.

Today, ask God for the courage to step beyond the boundaries of your self-doubts. Ask Him to guide you to a place where you can realize your full potential—a place where you are freed from the fear of failure. Ask Him to do His part, and promise Him that you will do your part. Don't ask Him to lead you to a "safe" place; ask Him to lead you to the "right" place . . . and remember: those two places are seldom the same.

He shall cover you with His feathers, And under His wings you shall take refuge; His truth shall be your shield and buckler. You shall not be afraid of the terror by night, Nor of the arrow that flies by day, Nor of the pestilence that walks in darkness, Nor of the destruction that lays waste at noonday. A thousand may fall at your side, And ten thousand at your right hand; But it shall not come near you.

PSALM 91:4-7 NKJV

Say to those who are fearful-hearted, "Be strong, do not fear! Behold, your God will come with vengeance, With the recompense of God; He will come and save you."

ISAIAH 35:4 NKJV

Have I not commanded you? Be strong and of good courage; do not be afraid, nor be dismayed, for the Lord your God is with you wherever you go."

JOSHUA 1:9 NKJV

The Lord is my light and my salvation; Whom shall I fear? The Lord is the strength of my life; Of whom shall I be afraid?

PSALM 27:1 NKJV

If a person fears God, he or she has no reason to fear anything else. On the other hand, if a person does not fear God, then fear becomes a way of life.

BETH MOORE

God alone can give us songs in the night.

C. H. SPURGEON

Fear lurks in the shadows of every area of life.
The future may look very threatening.
Jesus says, "Stop being afraid. Trust me!"

CHARLES SWINDOLL

He that fears not the future may enjoy the present.

THOMAS FULLER

Hope is some extraordinary spiritual grace that God gives us to control our fears, not to oust them.

VINCENT MCNABB

Additional Bible Readings

MATTHEW 6:34A; MATTHEW 8:26, 27; PROVERBS 3:24-26; PSALM 34:4

FINANCIAL DIFFICULTIES

The quest for financial security is a journey that leads us across many peaks and through a few unexpected valleys. When we celebrate life's great victories, we find it easy to praise God and to give thanks. But, when we find ourselves in the dark valleys of life, when we face disappointments or financial hardships, it's much more difficult to trust God's perfect plan. But, trust Him we must.

As Christians, we can be comforted: Whether we find ourselves at the pinnacle of the mountain or the darkest depths of the valley, God is there. And we Christians have every reason to live courageously. After all, Christ has already won the ultimate battle on the cross at Calvary. Still, even dedicated believers may find their courage tested by the inevitable setbacks and disappointments that accompany life here on earth. And you are no exception.

Will regular readings of your Bible make you a financial genius? Probably not. The Bible is God's Holy Word; it is intended not as a tool for prosperity, but as a tool for salvation. Nevertheless, the Bible can teach you how to become a more disciplined, patient person. As you become a more disciplined person in other aspects of your life, you will also become more disciplined in the management of your personal finances—and the following common-sense tips can help:

1. Enhance your earning power and keep enhancing your earning power: Opportunities to learn are limitless, and change is inevitable. In today's competitive workplace, those who stand still are, in reality, moving backwards . . . fast. (Proverbs 28:19)

2. Live within your means: Save money from every paycheck. Never spend more than you make. (Ecclesiastes 5:1)

3. Use credit wisely: Don't borrow money for things that rapidly go down in value (furniture, clothes, new cars, boats, etc.) And if you borrow money for things that are likely to go up (like your home), borrow only the amount that you can comfortably afford to repay (in other words, don't "max out" your mortgage!) (Proverbs 22:7)

4. Don't buy impulsively: Savvy salespeople want you to buy "right now." But savvy buyers take their time. (Proverbs 21:5)

5. Don't fall in love with "stuff." We live in a society that worships "stuff"—don't fall into that trap. Remember this: "stuff" is highly overrated. Worship God almighty, not the almighty dollar. (Proverbs 11:28)

6. Make sure that everybody in your family understands financial common sense. Within families, financial security is a team sport; make sure that everybody is on the team. (Matthew 12:25)

7. Give back to the Lord: God is the giver of all things good. What does He ask in return? A tiny ten percent. Don't withhold it from Him. (Malachi 3:10)

Give, and it will be given to you: good measure, pressed down,
shaken together, and running over will be put into your bosom.
For with the same measure that you use,
it will be measured back to you."

LUKE 6:38 NKJV

"Bring to the storehouse a full tenth of what you earn so there
will be food in my house. Test me in this,"
says the Lord All-Powerful. "I will open the windows
of heaven for you and pour out all the blessings you need."

MALACHI 3:10 NCV

Honor the Lord with your wealth and the firstfruits from
all your crops. Then your barns will be full,
and your wine barrels will overflow with new wine.

PROVERBS 3:9, 10 NCV

And my God shall supply all your need according to
His riches in glory by Christ Jesus.

PHILIPPIANS 4:19 NKJV

The first step in financial peace is saving money.
It's a straightforward thing.
Saving money must become a priority.

DAVE RAMSEY

If the Living Logos of God has the power to create and
sustain the universe… He is more than able to sustain
your marriage and your ministry, your faith and
your finances, your hope, and your health.

ANNE GRAHAM LOTZ

Economy is half the battle of life; it is not so hard
to earn money as it is to spend it well.

C. H. SPURGEON

Budgeting is telling your money where to go instead of
asking it where it went.

JOHN MAXWELL

God is entitled to a portion of our income.
Not because he needs it, but because we need to give it.

JAMES DOBSON

Additional Bible Readings

2 CORINTHIANS 9:6-8; DEUTERONOMY 28:3-8; DEUTERONOMY 8:7-18;

MATTHEW 6:31-33; PSALM 23:1; PSALM 34:1; PSALM 34:9, 10

HEALTH PROBLEMS

The American Theologian Reinhold Niebuhr composed a profoundly simple verse that has come to be known as the Serenity Prayer: "God, grant me the serenity to accept the things I cannot change, the courage to change the things I can, and the wisdom to know the difference."

Niebuhr's words are particularly important when we encounter health problems. Whenever we face health challenges, we should seek God's guidance as we struggle to accept the things that we cannot change, yet we should also strive mightily to change the things that we can change.

If you, or someone you love, is facing a health-related challenge, there are certainly things that you can control, and here are a few Biblically-based tips that can help:

Never lose sight of God's promises: God's survival guide, the Holy Bible, contains promises that can offer you courage and hope. Trust God's promises. (Hebrews 10:36)

Remember: it's almost never too late to improve your health: Consider a more healthy lifestyle as a form of worship. When God described your body as a temple, He wasn't kidding. Show your respect for God's Word by keeping your temple in tip-top shape. (1 Corinthians 6:19, 20)

Be proactive about your health: Don't sit around and wait for things to get worse; search for the best help you can find, and start that search now. (Proverbs 27:12)

View your journey to improved health as a spiritual journey, too. And the more spiritual growth you experience, the better. (2 Peter 3:18)

Remember: Life is a gift—health must be earned. You can enhance your health by cultivating sensible habits and by attending to your medical needs sooner rather than later. (Ephesians 4:1)

Perhaps this is the right time for you to commit yourself to a more sensible lifestyle. If so, then you'll need to take a close look at the way you eat, the way you exercise, and the way that you prioritize matters of life and health. Remember: the surest way to revolutionize your physical health is to revolutionize your habits.

And, if you've encountered unfortunate health circumstances that are, for the moment, beyond your power to control, accept those circumstances . . . and trust God. When you do, you can be comforted in the knowledge that your Creator is both loving and wise, and that He understands His plans perfectly, even when you do not.

---

*"Father, if it is Your will, take this cup away from Me;
nevertheless not My will, but Yours, be done."*

LUKE 22:42 NKJV

*But I discipline my body and bring it into subjection,
lest, when I have preached to others,
I myself should become disqualified.*

1 CORINTHIANS 9:27 NKJV

Is anyone among you suffering? Let him pray.

JAMES 5:13 NKJV

*A happy heart is like good medicine,
but a broken spirit drains your strength.*

PROVERBS 17:22 NCV

Jesus Christ is the One by Whom, for Whom, through Whom everything was made. Therefore, He knows what's wrong in your life and how to fix it.

ANNE GRAHAM LOTZ

God helps the sick in two ways, through the science of medicine and through the science of faith and prayer.

NORMAN VINCENT PEALE

The best way to show my gratitude to God is to accept everything, even my problems, with joy.

MOTHER TERESA

Jesus loved the will of His Father. He embraced the limitations, the necessities, the conditions, the very chains of his humanity as he walked and worked here on earth, fulfilling moment by moment His divine commission and the stern demands of His incarnation.
Never was there a world or even a look of complaint.

ELISABETH ELLIOT

Additional Bible Readings

MATTHEW 9:22; 2 KINGS 20:5; PROVERBS 3:5, 6; PHILIPPIANS 2:13;

1 CHRONICLES 19:13

JOB LOSS

Whether we like it or not, we live in a highly competitive global economy. And whether we like it or not, our jobs, like the ever-changing world in which we live, are in a constant state of flux.

Losing one's job can be a traumatic experience. Job loss is usually a problem of the first magnitude, a problem that results in financial and emotional stress. But of this we can be certain: Hidden beneath every problem is the seed of a solution—God's solution. Our challenge, as faithful believers, is to trust God's providence and seek His solutions. When we do, we eventually discover that God does nothing without a very good reason: His reason.

If you've recently experienced a job loss, here are some things to consider and some things to do:

1. Remember that God is still right here: He rules the mountaintops of life and the valleys, so don't lose hope. (Lamentations 3:25, 26)

2. If you're feeling sorry for yourself, stop: Self-pity isn't going to help you find a better job or build a better life. (2 Timothy 1:7)

3. If you're out of a job, you have a critically important job: finding a new one. Don't delay; don't take an extended vacation; don't try to improve your golf game; don't watch daytime TV. If you need a new job, you should spend at least 40 hours a week looking for it. And you should keep doing so until you find the job you need. (1 Chronicles 28:20)

4. Use all available tools. Those tools include, but are not limited to, friends, family, church members, former business associates, classified advertisements, employment services, the Internet, and your own shoe leather. (2 Peter 1:5, 6)

5. Think positive thoughts. Think positively about yourself, your abilities, and your future. After all, if you don't believe in those things, how can you expect your future employer to believe in them, either? (Philippians 4:8)

And he said: "The Lord is my rock and my fortress and
my deliverer; the God of my strength, in whom I will trust."

2 SAMUEL 22:2, 3 NKJV

"Be strong and brave, and do the work. Don't be afraid
or discouraged, because the Lord God, my God, is with you.
He will not fail you or leave you."

1 CHRONICLES 28:20 NCV

Come to Me, all you who labor and are heavy laden,
and I will give you rest. Take My yoke upon you and learn from
Me, for I am gentle and lowly in heart, and you will find rest
for your souls. For My yoke is easy and My burden is light.

MATTHEW 11:28-30 NKJV

Whatever your hand finds to do, do it with your might.

ECCLESIASTES 9:10 NKJV

More Thoughts About . . . JOB LOSS

Do not be afraid, then, that if you trust, or tell others to trust, the matter will end there. Trust is only the beginning and the continual foundation. When we trust Him, the Lord works, and His work is the important part of the whole matter.

HANNAH WHITALL SMITH

Waiting is the hardest kind of work, but God knows best, and we may joyfully leave all in His hands.

LOTTIE MOON

Great relief and satisfaction can come from seeking God's priorities for us in each season, discerning what is "best" in the midst of many noble opportunities, and pouring our most excellent energies into those things.

BETH MOORE

It is not work that's kills, but worry. And, it is amazing how much wear and tear the human mind and spirit can stand if it is free from friction and well-oiled by the Spirit.

VANCE HAVNER

Additional Bible Readings

1 CORINTHIANS 3:8; 2 TIMOTHY 2:15; JOHN 14:27; PSALM 31:14, 15;

PSALM 62:8

Loss of Meaning and Purpose

"Why did God put me here?" It's an easy question to ask and, at times, a very difficult question to answer. As you seek to answer that question, you should begin by remembering this: You are here because God put you here, and He has important work for you to do. But God's purposes will not always be clear to you. Sometimes you may wander aimlessly in a wilderness of your own making. And sometimes, you may struggle mightily against God in a vain effort to find success and happiness through your own means, not His.

Whenever we struggle against God's plans, we suffer. When we resist God's calling, our efforts bear little fruit. Our best strategy, therefore, is to seek God's wisdom and to follow Him wherever He chooses to lead. When we do so, we are blessed.

When we align ourselves with God's purposes, we avail ourselves of His power and His peace. But how can we know precisely what God's intentions are? The answer, of course, is that even the most well-intentioned believers face periods of uncertainty and doubt about the direction of their lives. So, too, will you.

When you arrive at one of life's inevitable crossroads, that is precisely the moment when you should turn your thoughts and prayers toward God. When you do, He will make Himself known to you in a time and manner of His choosing.

Are you earnestly seeking to discern God's purpose for your life? If so, remember these three points:

1. God has a plan for your life: If you believe that your life has no meaning, you are very wrong. God isn't finished with you yet, and He still has meaningful work for you to do. (Jeremiah 29:11)

2. If you seek God's plan sincerely and prayerfully, you will find it: God's plan for you may not be obvious, but neither is it incomprehensible. With prayer and patience, you can determine, with a surprising degree of clarity, the path that God intends for you to take. (Psalm 16:11)

3. When you discover God's purpose for your life, you will experience abundance, peace, joy, and power—God's power. And that's the only kind of power that really matters. (John 10:10; Psalm 84:5)

---

*God chose you to be his people, so I urge you now to live
the life to which God called you.*

EPHESIANS 4:1 NCV

*There is one thing I always do. Forgetting the past
and straining toward what is ahead, I keep trying to reach
the goal and get the prize for which God called me . . . .*

PHILIPPIANS 3:13, 14 NCV

*And let us not grow weary while doing good,
for in due season we shall reap if we do not lose heart.*

GALATIANS 6:9 NKJV

*May He grant you according to your heart's desire,
and fulfill all your purpose.*

PSALM 20:4 NKJV

Let your fellowship with the Father and with the Lord
Jesus Christ have as its one aim and object a life of quiet,
determined, unquestioning obedience.

ANDREW MURRAY

Only God's chosen task for you will ultimately satisfy.
Do not wait until it is too late to realize the privilege of
serving Him in His chosen position for you.

BETH MOORE

The really committed leave the safety of the harbor,
accept the risk of the open seas of faith, and set their
compasses for the place of total devotion to God and
whatever life adventures He plans for them.

BILL HYBELS

You were made by God and for God—
and until you understand that, life will not make sense.

RICK WARREN

Continually restate to yourself what the purpose
of your life is.

OSWALD CHAMBERS

Additional Bible Readings

ECCLESIASTES 3:1; JOHN 16:23, 24; PSALM 121; ROMANS 8:28

MATERIALISM

Thomas Carlyle observed, "Man is a tool-using animal; without tools he is nothing, with tools he is all." Carlyle understood that mankind depends upon a wide assortment of material goods to provide ease, comfort, security, and entertainment. Our material possessions improve our lives in countless ways, but when those possessions begin to assert undo control over our daily affairs, it's time to declare "Enough stuff!"

Whenever a person becomes absorbed with the acquisition of things, complications arise. Each new acquisition costs money or time, often both. To further complicate matters, many items can be purchased, not with real money, but with the something much more insidious: debt. Debt—especially consumer debt used to purchase depreciating assets—is a modern-day form of indentured servitude.

If you're looking for a sure-fire, time-tested way to simplify your life and thereby improve your world, learn to control your possessions before they control you. Purchase only those things that make a significant contribution to your well-being and the well-being of your family. Never spend more than you make. Understand the folly in buying consumer goods on credit. Never use credit cards as a way of financing your lifestyle.

Ask yourself this simple question: "Do I own my possessions, or do they own me?" If you don't like the answer you receive, make an iron-clad promise to stop acquiring and start divesting. As you simplify your life, you'll be amazed at the things you can do without. You be pleasantly surprised at the sense of satisfaction that accompanies your new-found moderation. And you'll understand first-hand that when it comes to material possessions, less truly is more.

How important are our material possessions? Not as important as we might think. In the lives of committed Christians, material possessions should play a rather small role. Of course, we all need the basic necessities of life, but once we meet those needs for ourselves and for our families, the piling up of possessions creates more problems than it solves. Our real riches, of course, are not of this world. We are never really rich until we are rich in spirit.

Martin Luther observed, "Many things I have tried to grasp and have lost. That which I have placed in God's hands I still have." His words apply to all of us. Our earthly riches are transitory; our spiritual riches are not.

Do you find yourself wrapped up in the concerns of the material world? If so, it's time to reorder your priorities by turning your thoughts and your prayers to more important matters. And, it's time to begin storing up riches that will endure throughout eternity: the spiritual kind.

For the love of money is a root of all kinds of evil,
for which some have strayed from the faith in their greediness,
and pierced themselves through with many sorrows. But you,
O man of God, flee these things and pursue righteousness,
godliness, faith, love, patience, gentleness.

1 TIMOTHY 6:10, 11 NKJV

Keep your lives free from the love of money,
and be satisfied with what you have.

HEBREWS 13:5 NCV

Serving God does make us very rich, if we are satisfied
with what we have. We brought nothing into the world,
so we can take nothing out. But, if we have food and clothes,
we will be satisfied with that.

1 TIMOTHY 6:6–8 NCV

No one can serve two masters. The person will hate one master
and love the other, or will follow one master and refuse to follow
the other. You cannot serve both God and worldly riches.

MATTHEW 6:24 NCV

If you want to be truly happy, you won't find it on
an endless quest for more stuff. You'll find it in receiving
God's generosity and then passing that generosity along.

BILL HYBELS

Hold everything earthly with a loose hand,
but grasp eternal things with a deathlike grip.

C. H. SPURGEON

Great wealth is not related to money! It is an attitude
of satisfaction coupled with inner peace.

CHARLES SWINDOLL

He is no fool who gives what he cannot keep to gain
what he cannot lose.

JIM ELLIOT

When the apostle Paul met Christ, he realized everything
in his asset column was actually a liability.
He found that Christ was all he needed.

JOHN MACARTHUR

Additional Bible Readings

LUKE 12:15; LUKE 12:19, 21; LUKE 12:34; MARK 8:36, 37;

MATTHEW 6:25, 26; PROVERBS 11:28

PRIORITIES
AND BALANCE

On your daily to-do list, all items are not created equal: Certain tasks are extremely important while others are not. Therefore, it's imperative that you prioritize your daily activities and complete each task in the approximate order of its importance.

The principle of doing first things first is simple in theory but more complicated in practice. Well-meaning family, friends, and coworkers have a way of making unexpected demands upon your time. Furthermore, each day has it own share of minor emergencies; these urgent matters tend to draw your attention away from more important ones. On paper, prioritizing is simple, but to act upon those priorities in the real world requires maturity, patience, determination, and balance.

If you fail to prioritize your day, life will automatically do the job for you. So your choice is simple: prioritize or be prioritized. It's a choice that will help determine the quality of your life.

If you're having trouble balancing the many demands of everyday living, perhaps you've been trying to organize your life according to your own plans, not God's. A better strategy, of course, is to take your daily obligations and place them in the hands of the One who created you. To do so, you must prioritize your day according to God's commandments, and you must seek His will and His wisdom in all matters. Then, you can face the coming day with the assurance that the same God who created our universe out of nothingness will help you place first things first in your own life.

Are you living a balanced life that allows time for worship, for family, for work, for exercise, and a little time left over for you? Or do you feel overworked, under-appreciated, overwhelmed, and underpaid? If your to-do list is "maxed out" and your energy is on the wane, it's time to restore a sense of balance to your life. You can do so by turning the concerns and the priorities of this day over to God—prayerfully, earnestly, and often. Then, you must listen for His answer . . . and trust the answer He gives.

*Come to Me, all you who labor and are heavy laden, and
I will give you rest. Take My yoke upon you and learn from
Me, for I am gentle and lowly in heart, and you will find rest
for your souls. For My yoke is easy and My burden is light.*

MATTHEW 11:28-30 NKJV

*But those who wait on the Lord Shall renew their strength;
They shall mount up with wings like eagles,
They shall run and not be weary, They shall walk and not faint.*

ISAIAH 40:31 NKJV

*The thing you should want most is God's kingdom
and doing what God wants. Then all these other things
you need will be given to you.*

MATTHEW 6:33 NCV

*So teach us to number our days,
that we may gain a heart of wisdom.*

PSALM 90:12 NKJV

We move through life in such a distracted way
that we do not even take the time to wonder if any
of the things we think, say, or do are worth
thinking, saying, or doing.

HENRI NOUWEN

Never give up on the important things.
Never worry about the unimportant things.

MARIE T. FREEMAN

Putting first things first is an issue at the very heart of life.

STEPHEN COVEY

Balance wisely your professional life and your family life.
God only allows us so many opportunities with
our children to read a story, to go fishing, to play catch,
and to say our prayers together.
Try not to miss a single one of them.

JAMES DOBSON

Additional Bible Readings

1 CORINTHIANS 9:24, 25; HEBREWS 12:1, 2; MATTHEW 7:13, 14;

PHILIPPIANS 3:15, 16; PHILIPPIANS 4:8, 9

REPENTANCE

Who among us has sinned? All of us. But, God calls upon us to turn away from sin by following His commandments. And the good news is this: When we do ask for God's forgiveness and turn our hearts to Him, He forgives us absolutely and completely.

We cannot sin against God without consequence. We cannot live outside His will without injury. We cannot distance ourselves from God without hardening our hearts. We cannot yield to the ever-tempting distractions of our world and, at the same time, enjoy God's peace.

Sometimes, in a futile attempt to justify our behaviors, we make a distinction between "big" sins and "little" ones. To do so is a mistake of "big" proportions. Sins of all shapes and sizes have the power to do us great harm. And in a world where sin is big business, that's certainly a sobering thought.

Genuine repentance requires more than simply offering God apologies for our misdeeds. Real repentance may start with feelings of sorrow and remorse, but it ends only when we turn away from the sin that has heretofore distanced us from our Creator. In truth, we offer our most meaningful apologies to God, not with our words, but with our actions. As long as we are still engaged in sin, we may be "repenting," but we have not fully "repented."

God's Word teaches that when we invite Christ to rule over our lives, we become new beings:

"You were taught to leave your old self—to stop living the evil way you lived before. That old self becomes worse, because people are fooled by the evil things they want to do. But you were taught to be made new in your hearts, to become a new person. That new person is made to be like God—made to be truly good and holy."

EPHESIANS 4:22–24 NCV

Is there an aspect of your life that is preventing you from becoming a new person in Christ? Are you engaged in an activity that is distancing you from your God? If so, ask for His forgiveness, and—just as importantly—stop sinning. Then, wrap yourself in the protection of God's Word. When you do, you will be secure.

So this is what the Lord says: "If you change your heart and return to me, I will take you back. Then you may serve me. And if you speak things that have worth, not useless words, then you may speak for me.

JEREMIAH 15:19 NCV

He who covers his sins will not prosper, but whoever confesses and forsakes them will have mercy.

PROVERBS 28:13 NKJV

Come near to God, and God will come near to you. You sinners, clean sin out of your lives. You who are trying to follow God and the world at the same time, make your thinking pure.

JAMES 4:8 NCV

If My people who are called by My name will humble themselves, and pray and seek My face, and turn from their wicked ways, then I will hear from heaven, and will forgive their sin and heal their land.

2 CHRONICLES 7:14 NKJV

True confession of sin is not just with the lips,
for there must also be a broken heart.

WARREN WIERSBE

Repentance removes old sins and wrong attitudes,
and it opens the way for the Holy Spirit to restore
our spiritual health.

SHIRLEY DOBSON

In terms of the parable of the Prodigal Son, repentance is
the flight home that leads to joyful celebration. It opens
the way to a future, to a relationship restored.

PHILIP YANCEY

Repentance involves a radical change of heart and mind
in which we agree with God's evaluation of our sin and
then take specific action to align ourselves with His will.

HENRY BLACKABY

When true repentance comes, God will not hesitate for
a moment to forgive, cast the sins in the sea of
forgetfulness, and put the child on the road to restoration.

BETH MOORE

Additional Bible Readings

1 JOHN 1:9; ACTS 26:20; LUKE 5:30-32; PSALM 34:18; ROMANS 6:17

AFTER THE CRISIS

"For I will restore health to you and heal you of your wounds,"
says the Lord.

JEREMIAH 30:17 NKJV

Perhaps you have picked up this book during a time of personal crisis. If so, you have turned to the right place: the wisdom of God's Holy Word. And sometime soon, perhaps sooner than you expect, the clouds will part, the sun will shine, and your crisis will pass. But the passing of your personal crisis *does not* mean that your spiritual journey has reached its completion. Far from it!

The path to spiritual maturity unfolds day by day. Each day offers the opportunity to worship God, to ignore God, or to rebel against God. When you worship Him with your prayers, your words, your thoughts, and your actions, you will be blessed by the richness of your relationship with the Father.

Today, and every day after it, presents fresh opportunities for spiritual growth. If you choose, you can seize those opportunities by obeying God's Word, by seeking His will, and by walking with His Son. And as you begin your life "after the crisis," here are a few things to remember:

1. Learn the lessons; make the changes: Every crisis has lessons to teach. Your job is to learn those lessons *and* to make the necessary changes that *prove* you've learned those lessons. (Proverbs 9:9)

2. Remember that the healing continues after the crisis has passed: After a major life crisis, don't expect instantaneous healing—expect a few emotional aftershocks. From time to time, you may find yourself dwelling *on* the past—but don't dwell *in* the past. And if your emotional aftershocks become too intense, seek help. (Psalm 27:14)

3. Get connected; get involved: After the crisis, it will be your responsibility to engage yourself with people and organizations that provide the enrichment and support you need. Whether it's your local church, a neighborhood service organization, or a local support group, get involved: you need *their* help . . . and *they* need yours. (1 Thessalonians 5:11)

4. If the problem recurs, you'll be better prepared when it does: sometimes, Old Man Trouble has a way of rearing his head over and over again. But if Mister Trouble *does* return to your house, you can take comfort in the fact that after this crisis, you are now better prepared to meet him, to greet him, and to usher him out the door . . . quickly! (Hebrews 12:11)